Teaching Re Mental Healtn Across the Curriculum

Written by a teacher for teachers, *Teaching Resilience and Mental Health Across the Curriculum* is an integrative approach to pedagogy for educators at the high school and college level to survive, thrive, and sustain in the profession. Blending theory, research, and practice for a comprehensive program for teachers to incorporate well-being tools into the classroom, each of the book's five foundations includes engaging information, strategies, real-world examples, interactive reflection questions, and activities that can be directly applied to teaching and life.

Practical guidance in designing a real-world curriculum is offered alongside accessible strategies for engagement, investment, and active learning in student-centered classrooms. An essential guide for teachers, it includes techniques for incorporating well-being that are grounded in culturally responsive teaching, trauma-informed instruction, mental health, resilience, and emotional literacy. Teachers will also gain insight on how to make the career sustainable through practices for self-compassion and authentic self-care so they can not only survive, but flourish in and out of school. For all the challenges that students and teachers face, this book defines what it means, and what it takes, to teach in today's classrooms.

Linda Yaron Weston is the author of *Mindfulness for Young Adults: Tools to Thrive in School and Life*. A National Board Certified Teacher with twenty years of classroom experience teaching academic and well-being courses at the high school and college level, she lectures at the University of Southern California, where she developed their undergraduate mindfulness course. Across grade levels, she regularly leads professional development for educators on how to integrate mindfulness and well-being supports in the classroom.

Teaching Resilience and Mental Health Across the Curriculum

A Guide for High School and College Teachers

Linda Yaron Weston

Routledge
Taylor & Francis Group

NEW YORK AND LONDON

Cover image: © Getty Images

First published 2023
by Routledge
605 Third Avenue, New York, NY 10158

and by Routledge
4 Park Square, Milton Park, Abingdon, Oxon, OX14 4RN

Routledge is an imprint of the Taylor & Francis Group, an informa business

© 2023 Linda Yaron Weston

ISBN: 978-1-032-33148-5 (hbk)
ISBN: 978-1-032-33139-3 (pbk)
ISBN: 978-1-003-31840-8 (ebk)

DOI: 10.4324/9781003318408

Typeset in Palatino
by SPi Technologies India Pvt Ltd (Straive)

For Dave
For BW
For teachers, who inspire and uplift us all

Contents

Meet the Author

Linda Yaron Weston is the author of *Mindfulness for Young Adults: Tools to Thrive in School and Life*. A National Board Certified Teacher with two decades of classroom experience teaching academic and well-being courses at the high school and college level, she lectures at the University of Southern California, where she developed their under-graduate mindfulness course. She holds dual master's degrees in education from UCLA, bachelor's degrees in human development and literatures of the world from UC San Diego, teaching credentials in English, physical education and health, and certifications in mindfulness and yoga. Her depth of expertise contributes to an integrative, interdisciplinary approach to teaching that blends theory, research, and practice. Through her career, she has worked to increase opportunities for students to thrive, particularly around the areas of student engagement, equity and access, mental and physical health, and school and community partnerships. As a public high school English teacher, she designed and led real-world learning experiences, including a student art exhibition and presentation at the Department of Education in Washington, D.C. and a student photography exhibition on self-portraiture in partnership with The Getty Center and 826LA. Across grade levels, she regularly leads professional development for educators on how to integrate mindfulness and well-being supports in the classroom. She served as a U.S. Department of Education Teaching Ambassador Fellow where she engaged in federal education policy, as well as in the Fulbright Hays Seminars Abroad Program and U.S. State Department Teachers for Global Classrooms Program.

Acknowledgements

Thank you to my mom for being my very first teacher. I carry your lessons with me.

To my publisher at Routledge, Lauren Davis, and editorial assistant, Julia Giordano, for their efforts and support in helping bring this book into the world.

To the teachers who have shaped my journey. It is because of your care that I made it.

To my teaching mentors who nurtured my growth and showed me what it meant to care for all students.

To my teaching colleagues and friends who have made this job so much better because of you. It is not an easy thing to be a teacher with all that is called for and the conditions that exist. I couldn't have survived in the profession without you.

To my students, who uplift and inspire me each day to want to be a better teacher.

And, most of all, to my incredible husband Dave. You are my home and my heart. And to BW, who has brought so much joy already.

Introduction

What does it mean and what does it take to not only survive in the classroom, but to thrive and sustain in the profession? Educators are called on to do increasingly more, without adequate time, resources, conditions, or compensation. It is hard enough, and these times have made it all that much harder.

When I recently asked a former mentee how she was doing, she replied, "Just the usual end of semester burnout." Another colleague I spoke with on her first day of winter break was in tears reflecting on what she endured that semester. Though stress, burnout, and the high toll of the job are often normalized, there should be nothing normal about burnout. Again and again, I hear of amazing educators who leave the profession because the conditions were unsustainable. Students too are stressed, anxious, struggling with mental health, and unable to focus in the classroom. I say this not to discourage you, but to bring to the forefront the importance of systemically integrating well-being supports alongside academics so that students and teachers can thrive.

My past twenty years teaching academic and well-being courses at the high school and college level has given me unique insight into the foundations of engagement, resilience, and mental health in teaching young adults. It's defined my integrative approach to aligning well-being supports alongside academics so that students and teachers can flourish. This is not to remove responsibility from systems for bettering the conditions of our schools. And this is not to add to teacher's already full plates, or for them to carry the weight of it on their shoulders, or to assume that telling them to do more personal self-care will fix systemic issues. But to say that in the midst of challenging circumstances, there are things we can do to make schools healthier and more nourishing places to teach and learn.

This book offers an integrative approach to teaching in a way that is engaging, responsive, student-centered, and honors the cultures and identities of the students we teach. It isn't an add-on—it's a reframing toward a more culturally relevant, emotionally responsive, trauma-sensitive approach to schooling. This is not separate from teaching—this is what it means to teach in today's classrooms. For the particular challenges that students of color face, teaching in this way is not separate from a social justice pedagogy of equity and access—it is an essential part of one. And it's within a framework of rigorous curriculum design where goals, instruction, and assessment are aligned and sequenced toward student learning.

It's personal to me. After thirteen years, my career teaching high school English ended with me in the hospital less than a month before the school year finished. This was despite all I did to promote well-being: teaching yoga, creating a Healthy Lifestyles elective course, earning physical education and health credentials, teaching units on childhood obesity, facilitating wellness professional development for teachers, leading a staff health challenge. Three years earlier, a trip to India triggered an autoimmune condition that I then tried to manage while teaching. I was at the peak of my career—facilitating community partnerships, serving in teacher leadership positions, developing professional development courses, publishing education articles, and rocking in the classroom with a real-world project-based curriculum. I had tried to make it as sustainable as I could, but there was no way around it. Stress compromises the immune system. I wanted to be in it for the long run, but with the conditions of schooling as they are, and my body shouting at me, in the end it wasn't my choice to make.

And so, the next chapter of my career blended my passions for well-being and education. I was hired to teach Yoga and Stress Management for Healthy Living courses at the University of Southern California and went on to develop their Introduction to Mindfulness undergraduate course program, which has grown to serve 190 students each semester across ten course sections and five instructors. I wrote the curriculum book *Mindfulness for Young Adults: Tools to Thrive in School and Life*, led professional development for educators, districts, and organizations, and got clearer on what it meant for me to teach and how I wanted to serve the profession.

In speaking with others about including well-being supports alongside academics, though there was agreement that there was an urgent need, there seemed to be a gap what it looked like in a practical, integrated approach. And that's how this book came to be. Where my first book *Mindfulness for Young Adults* is the what, *Teaching Resilience and Mental Health Across the Curriculum* is the how.

This book is an attempt to share not just how to survive in the classroom, but to thrive and sustain in it. It includes sections for curriculum design alongside ones for nurturing our minds, bodies, and hearts, including managing emotions and stressors of the job, and self-compassion practices for those times when we might feel like we are not enough. This book is a blueprint for what it looks like to situate well-being alongside academics in the classroom—not as a separate thing, but as an integrated vehicle for building engagement, investment, and community. It is a way of caring for ourselves and our students so that we can all thrive in school and life.

This book is for teachers at the high school and college level who want to learn what it means to create thriving classroom environments where students are at the center of their learning experience and where they can navigate the stresses of the job and flourish. For as rigorous and difficult as it often is to teach in schooling conditions, I hope the topics in this book are part of the dialogue in teacher and leadership preparation programs exploring how to make the job more sustainable and how to integrate well-being supports across the curriculum and profession.

Considering all the training and professional development that k-12 teachers do to prepare to teach, I was surprised by the absence of sufficient or required training in higher ed. It is a very different thing to be an expert in a subject area and then to teach that subject in a curriculum that aligns goals, instruction, and assessment in a way that is engaging, relevant, and meaningful for students in a safe and supportive classroom environment. Perhaps college students may be more adaptable or may not resist a lecture-based class the way my high school students would have, but they certainly notice, appreciate, and benefit from a supportive and meaningful classroom experience. I hope this book can be a useful resource for designing and supporting rich college classroom experiences for students and helping teachers thrive there too.

Teaching young adults is particularly dynamic as they are discovering who they are and the individuals they will become. They grapple with what it means to be human and alive and what they want their lives to mean. They need structure and boundaries, and yet at the same time the independence and freedom to explore. They require the room to take risks and figure things out on their own, and the guidance of what to do when they fall. They will test and cross boundaries. They want to be inspired and to know that they matter and can have an impact in this world. They want to be seen, heard, and understood, just like all of us. And at the same time, their hoodie may cover their eyes, as if they aim to be invisible. They may experience love, a job, driving, drinking, substance use, sex for the first time. They may be transitioning out of the structure of mandatory schooling and making important life choices that will impact the opportunities and trajectory of their lives. Though they may seem too cool for help at times, the guidance and support of caring adults can make all the difference as they navigate what it means to live and learn in today's world.

I don't have all the answers. It's the posing of the questions, the dialogue within ourselves and with others, the trying over and over that gets us closer to what it takes for flourishing teaching and learning to occur.

Supporting educators and being alongside them as they lay the foundations of their teaching practice brings me deep joy. In mentoring teachers across subjects of English, history, math, science, and mindfulness, I've found that there are certain foundations that apply across the curriculum. Though examples and curriculum samples in this book lean on the particular subject areas I've taught—especially English, mindfulness, healthy living, and stress management—this book and these teaching practices aren't subject- or grade level-specific. As an early yoga teaching mentor, Annie, said to me, "good teaching is good teaching." It is my hope that sharing these foundations of teaching and learning may be of use to you as you explore what it means for you and your students to thrive in the classroom. Please take what works, modify to fit your needs and style, and leave the rest. Thank you for the work you do to inspire, uplift, and educate the next generation of young people. It is an honor to be on the journey with you.

Foundation 1: Purpose

Chapters 1: Purpose and 2: Investment set the conditions for building the resilience, responsiveness, and mental health discussed in later chapters. Student engagement and purposeful curriculum design are not separate from the discussion of socioemotional supports—they are included here as a foundational framework for the classroom conditions that facilitate building those skills.

What is your why?

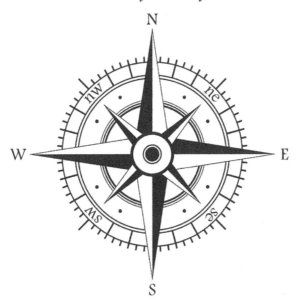

FIGURE 1.1

DOI: 10.4324/9781003318408-1

A. Find Your Why

Students need to know why they are doing what they are doing, that it is worth it to them, and that the person asking them to do it cares about their learning. If they are going to invest their time and effort and step outside their comfort zone, they need to know that it means something.

This involves getting clear on your what, how, and why of teaching.

What are students learning?
How will that content be taught so that it can be learned?
How will I know students are learning it?
Why does it matter?

Messaging and communicating the why builds investment and purpose. It helps them know that what they are doing is meaningful—to them, to you, to the world they are living in. That they matter and the work they do matters. Communicating learning goals with aligned messages enables students to clarify what they will learn, what skills they will build, and why it's important.

On the first day in my university mindfulness classroom, I ask students why they signed up for the course, and then why they might want to meditate. They meditate *so that* they can find a moment of stillness in the busyness of life, learn to be more responsive rather than reactive, feel more peace and ease within their day, learn to be more present in their lives, or countless other reasons they might take time to sit and breathe and be.

In my high school English classroom, this translated into communication skill building of reading, writing, speaking, and listening to increase opportunities to succeed. I wanted them to understand any material they are faced with, have the tools to analyze it for deeper meaning, respond and interact with it through written and oral communication, and sculpt verbal and written responses with attention to style and structure. The more they built their skills, the more powerful they would become and the more opportunities they would have. We talked about how language is power, knowledge is power, and what that power might mean for them, their families, their communities. For the times it seems like we're slogging along, we come back to that foundational question of "why are you here?" This places students at the center of their learning experience and helps them define for themselves what it means for them to be in the classroom, what they believe in, and what they want their learning experience and lives to be about.

Messages are constantly communicated in classrooms, whether unconsciously or intentionally. What are the messages being sent? What messages are received? What might get in the way of communicating these messages clearly? Years after being in my class, a student sent me a photo of a post-it note he kept that I wrote to him, "Juan, don't settle for being average. Be the best version of yourself—expect nothing less." This was a reminder of his why and the expectation that he can achieve it. He felt was important enough and clear enough of a message to keep with him and let me know that he still kept it.

Make it explicit, repeat it, ingrain it, and integrate it into the curriculum to unify a class and inspire a sense of purpose in students. My high school syllabus came to include the "17 Commitments" of messages I collected and borrowed through the years:

I started out teaching in a school with 5,500 students and a dropout rate of over half the student body. Only a fraction of students who graduated made it to and through college. Belen (unless otherwise noted, names have been changed to protect student privacy), a first-generation student in my ninth grade English class, and later Wellesley College graduate, Gates Millennium Scholar, and now medical student on her way to becoming a doctor, reflected about the impact of her approach to goals. "Having goals has allowed me to succeed. I've never been scared to aspire to do or become something, and believe my attitude of 'it doesn't hurt to try' has been the reason for my success." At an awards banquet her sophomore year of high school, she witnessed a classmate receive countless awards and decided she wanted to be just like her.

1. I can do it!
2. Never give up. Ever. If I fall, I stand up and keep walking.
3. Know my purpose. Be present and aware to direct what I think, say, and do toward my purpose.
4. Grow stronger. Knowledge is power. Language is power. With power comes responsibility.
5. Make it happen. What I put in is what I get out. The best way out is through. Find the way.
6. If I want what I've never had, I must do what I've never done. If I want a different result, I have to do things differently.
7. Everything I want is on the other side of fear. Lean into my edge.
8. I can't control the past, but I can control how I view it and what I do from this point forward. People and events only have the power I give them.
9. The way I do any one thing is the way I do everything.
10. I am the choices I make. Don't settle for being average—choose greatness.
11. Value my time. Ask if what I'm doing with my time is aligned with the life I want.
12. Growth mindset. The thing I practice is the thing that grows. Water the right seeds.
13. Leave it better than I found it. Make situations and spaces better because I'm in them.
14. Always keep my word. Do what I say I'm going to do and keep commitments.
15. Align my goals with my thoughts, words, and actions.
16. No one of us alone is as strong as all of us together. Be the change I want in my community.
17. Create multigenerational change. I have a supportive army of ancestors that stand beside me.

> I became determined to become a (Gates) Millennium Scholar, receive many awards, and be celebrated upon graduation. ... Having accomplished my goals in high school didn't signify the end of my endeavors but instead taught me that I work best when I have something to look forward to or something that I want to accomplish and that I work best with plans.

This is not to say that a goal solves everything, or to place an achievement ideology on students who are struggling in systems not designed for their success, or that systemic, ongoing educational inequities are cured by goals, but that it's an important component of success.

Just as seeing a classmate accomplish a goal made success tangible and believable for Belen, students need to see narratives of others who have made it, and the possibility of what that could mean for their lives. They need to know that what they put in is worth what they will get out. Teaching in urban high schools for most of my career, many of my students may not have personally known someone who graduated from college, or became a doctor, or lawyer. When they see it in others, they can believe that it is possible for them. It was important for me to bring people into my classroom who were in careers that students may not be exposed to. Former students also came back to share about their experiences in college. Students participated in internships where they met people in various industries. They went on fieldtrips to universities to sense what it is like to be on a college campus. This created a culture where success is more possible and tangible. Students claimed their goals and declared what it is they wanted to do and how they planned to get there.

Young adults who have a sense of purpose report higher happiness and health levels. According to researcher Kendall Cotton Bronk, purpose has four components: dedicated commitment, personal meaningfulness, goal-directedness, and a vision bigger than self. Purpose can anchor attention toward a meaningful goal and connect us to others who are in pursuit of similar ones.

As a teacher in college, my students now participate in panels where they can share their experiences with high school students and others. In sharing their stories and voices, they themselves benefit and become leaders and advocates of student voice and empowerment. A student, Ellie, reflected that participating in a panel "was an illuminating experience for me." Hearing the stories of the other panelists showed her how similar they all are in the battles they're facing. "It was also extremely moving that professionals wanted to hear about our experiences with mindfulness and seek our advice as students on ways they can incorporate mindfulness into their respective areas of expertise." She was proud to participate and felt the event gave her hope and had a positive impact on her and the other panelists.

As important as it is for students to find their why, it is for teachers too. Why are we doing this career? Why did we choose it? Beyond the money, fame, and glamour of the job (if only), why are we here? For the wide spectrum of high highs and low lows that come with teaching, finding your why will carry you through the tough times. In my high school classroom hung a poster of Martin Luther King, Jr. looking out of a Birmingham jail cell with the quote, "Your self-sacrificing devotion to your purpose in life and your unwavering faith will carry you through times of difficulty." Some days, it was more for me than my students.

Goals and Decisions

I constantly messaged the quotes, "If we want a different result, we have to do things differently" and "If we want what we've never had, we have to do what we've never done." Why are we here? What do they hope to get out of it? How can we align our goals with our actions? Research shows that goals are more achievable when they're specific, shared with others, and when we create our goals ourselves. We can clarify the intrinsic motivation of the goal of what we hope to gain from it on a deeper level. We can work a little every day toward our goals and celebrate the success of smaller goals.

Risky decision-making seems to peak in late teens and early twenties and is magnified in the presence of peers. The brain is still developing in decision-making areas of incentive processing and reward seeking. Knowing this, it can be helpful for young adults to clarify their purpose and bring more consciousness to decisions around goals. Mindfulness practices (explored in Chapter 4: Mental Health) can foster more awareness and power in making responsive, rather than reactive, choices.

It can be helpful for students to clarify if it's a short- or long-term goal. The SMART goals framework can be used to create goals that are **S**pecific, **M**easurable, **A**chievable, **R**ealistic, and within a **T**imeframe. I also have used the following framework with students in studying their goals and those of individuals in history and literature:

◆ *Situation*: What is your situation in relation to your goal?
◆ *Goal*: What are you trying to achieve?
◆ *Obstacles*: What obstacles (internal or external) may stand in your way?
◆ *Method*: How are you going to overcome obstacles and achieve your goal?
◆ *Assessment*: What is the outcome? How will you measure whether or not you have achieved your goal?

Classroom Application

A. Ask students: Why are you here? Why did you sign up for the class? What do you hope to get out of it?
B. Ask students: What is a long-term goal you have? Why is it important to you? What are the short-term goals that will help you achieve it? What might get in your way and how might you address this?
C. Create shared norms as a class. Ask students: What do you need so that you can thrive here?
D. Make a shared list of classroom commitments.
E. Invite a guest speaker to speak about a goal they achieved and how they did it.

Questions for Reflection or Discussion

1. What is your purpose or philosophy for teaching? What would students say is the purpose of your class?

2. Define your mission statement in 1–2 sentences. Have students define their mission statements.

3. Five years from now, what do you want students' biggest takeaways from your class to be?

B. Curriculum: Aligning Goals, Instruction, and Assessment

I was told early on that a good curriculum is the best classroom management. It still rings just as true for me today. What are the skills, themes, and content taught through the curriculum? How can it be taught in a way that students want to learn it? A strong curriculum will identify, articulate, and scaffold purpose. Through themes, skills, and experiences, students work toward shared and individual purpose-driven goals. Within that context, I aim to integrate resilience and mental health within the curriculum, not separate from the curriculum itself.

Ideally, goals are aligned with curriculum, are aligned with instruction, are aligned with assessment, and (for a gold star) are looped back into professional development. Some frameworks and models I've found helpful are included here:

Learning Goals

Learning objectives are the goals students achieve through the experiences in the course. These are measurable and achievable skills, knowledge, or dispositions that guide what is taught. The teacher is a facilitator who curates a learning experience and creates conditions for learning the classroom objectives. Various models can be helpful for creating learning goals that align with the intended amount of rigor.

Bloom's Taxonomy includes a hierarchy of learning processes listed below from simple to complex, as elaborated on in the revised version.

Remember: recall facts or basic concepts
Understand: explain ideas or concepts
Apply: use information in new situations
Analyze: draw conclusions among ideas
Evaluate: justify a stand or decisions
Create: produce new or original work

Webb's Depth of Knowledge can help determine the cognitive complexity of a learning goal.

Level 1: recall and reproduction (label, recall, repeat, define)

Level 2: skills and concepts (categorize, classify, infer, organize, predict)

Level 3: strategic thinking (critique, construct, assess, investigate)

Level 4: extended thinking (analyze, critique, apply, synthesize, design, create)

In a professional development for the Teachers for Global Classrooms program, we were asked, "What century are you preparing your students for?" Rapid changes in technology and innovation mean students will have jobs we can't even yet imagine. This has implications for what it means to be college- and career-ready with 21st century skills.

The Four Domains of Global Competence can help prepare students for the dynamic futures they will be stepping into.

1. *Investigate the world*: investigate the world beyond their immediate environment
2. *Recognize perspectives*: recognize their own and others' perspectives
3. *Communicate ideas*: communicate their ideas effectively with diverse audiences
4. *Take action*: translate their ideas into appropriate action to improve conditions

The Survey to Assess Global Competence includes questions for educators to keep in mind when assessing global competency and planning curricular units.

1. Knowledge about global issues: What do your students know about global issues, and how well do they know it?
   a) To what extent are students aware that global issues exist and affect their lives?

b) Are students studying a global issue in depth over a long period of time?

c) To what extent are students aware that global issues are interrelated, complex and challenging, and ever-changing?

d) To what extent are students aware that their information and knowledge on most global issues can be expanded, or could be deeper, and that they need to continue seeking information about how global issues are formed and influenced?

2. Skills regarding global issues: How are your students going to learn about issues?

a) To what extent do students know how to study about global issues? Do they have the skills needed to investigate and research a topic or issue, solve problems, analyze issues, interpret information, make a case for a point of view through reasoned persuasion?

b) To what extent do students know how to look for information about an issue? Do students know how to develop criteria for discriminating, evaluating, selecting, and responding to useful and relevant data? Do they know how to process the information that they have found? Do they know how to present their information to others?

c) To what extent do students have the ability to suspend judgment when confronted with new information about an issue when that information is in conflict with their own understandings and values?

Curriculum Design

Understanding by design or backwards planning models include starting with the end in mind. What skills, knowledge, or enduring understandings do we want students to achieve? And from that point determining the sequence and activities needed for students to get there.

Essential questions and meaningful themes help students see how a curriculum is relevant to their identities and lives. Essential questions are those that require deep exploration to uncover insights about our world, society, and the human condition. They do not have a simple yes or no answer, and they can unfold to meaningful classroom discussions. Over the years, some of my essential questions included:

What does it mean to stand for something?
What does it mean to be free?
Who am I and what are the things that make me who I am?

Sample units using these questions are included in Appendix A.

Project-Based Learning involves sequencing skills and component parts that build toward a project. It situates learning in the context of something bigger than an assignment, and involves working toward a goal. Some examples I've designed include a *Revolutionary Times* newspaper, a community art exhibition on identity, and a Ted Talk on from the perspective of a literary or historical figure. Through these projects, students built skills and worked on component parts that led to an event, large project, or performance to showcase their learning.

The *Into, Through, and Beyond* framework for lesson planning involves the activities that hook students into the curriculum, get them through it, and extend their learning beyond the lesson. Each class lesson or curricular unit has a beginning, middle, and end that will help achieve learning goals. When lesson planning, budget time to spending the most time on the most important things.

◆ *Beginning/Into*: the "into" of a lesson hooks students into what they will be doing. Why is this important? When do they receive what information? How are instructions given and received? The into builds investment, purpose, and clarity so that students can have what they need to make it through the learning experience.

◆ *Middle/Through*: this is where the learning happens and the exploration of activities to achieve learning goals. What activities are student doing? How are they doing it? How is their depth of learning facilitated? What questions and follow-up questions are needed for depth and rigor? What is the teacher doing as students are learning?

♦ _End/Beyond_: the "beyond" measures and extends learning past the lesson. How do we know that they've learned what we've wanted them to learn? What will they do with it? How do they share reflections about their learning?

KWL Charts (Know, Want to know, Learned) can be helpful for an informal check of student prior knowledge and generating curiosity about the topic. After the lesson, they reflect on what they learned:

What I know	What I want to know	What I learned

Ways of Learning
Active Learning
In active learning classrooms, students are engaged in the content and applying their knowledge. They are not passively receiving knowledge, but they interact with it, make sense of it, and apply it. In a teacher-centered classroom, the teacher gives the knowledge to students. A student-centered classroom meets students where they're at and gives them the tools and reasons to build their skills in relevant, real-world applications.

To measure this, teachers can look at what actions students are doing: asking questions, reflecting, discussing, problem solving, writing, speaking, etc. What is the nature of the task and how are they approaching it? What is the amount of time the teacher is talking versus the amount of time students are actively doing? What is the function of lecture and what is the mode of learning? For engagement, I try not to lecture for more than ten minutes at a time. The rest of classroom time is typically spent with students writing, reflecting, discussing in small and whole groups, and participating in activities.

Learning Styles
Students learn in different ways and likely have a dominant modality they learn best in. _Visual_ learners tend to learn by seeing,

auditory learners by listening, and *kinesthetic* learners by experiencing and doing. Students may have preferred learning styles for their inputs (information they take in), and the outputs (how they express their learning). People acquire and process information differently. Some may be independent learners, some social learners, and each learner may have a preferred motivational approach. Students learn best when we can incorporate multiple forms of learning styles into the classroom when giving instructions, providing content, designing activities, and assessing student learning through multiple measures.

Growth-Model Differentiation

One of the biggest challenges in a classroom is how to make a course equally rigorous for students who are all at different skill levels. Differentiating instruction entails reframing what we are instructing and approaching learning from a skills-based lens. The challenge is not to get everyone at the same level—it's how to maximally increase everyone's skills individually through a shared learning environment. We can maintain high and clear expectations, with differentiating supports to access them.

The Zone of Proximal Development is the distance between where a learner is at and where they can get to with adult guidance and support. Skillful curriculum design and application can take students from where they are to where they can grow to within the given learning experience.

A Yogic Lens in Differentiating Instruction

In my yoga teacher training we were taught to design skillful sequences and how to identify and sequence component parts needed to help students arrive at a peak pose, while giving clear instruction, feedback, and personalized adjustments to help students work with their unique bodies. Multiple modalities of learning are utilized as students hear instructions, see modeling of how the correct form of the pose looks, and then kinesthetically perform the pose with their own bodies. In a good yoga class, the instructor creates a safe, supported, and guided environment for students to explore and grow their own practice with assistance from the teacher. Designing and applying curriculum in the classroom isn't all that different.

Two types of yoga, Iyengar and ashtanga, come to mind when thinking of classroom structures. Iyengar is a therapeutic practice that involves many props. The support of props helps students achieve higher levels of practice and alignment when considering their own bodies. They are the classroom scaffolds that teachers learn how, where, and when to place when differentiating instruction. In ashtanga, each student completes his or her own individualized plan of practice given by the instructor. The room may be silent, save the sound of breath, as each practitioner moves at an individual pace and practice. Both styles can be applied to the classroom, as teachers individually differentiate instruction, know student needs, build on individual strengths, and guide students toward goals in a supported practice to help them grow.

One day in a yoga instructor training, our cohort gathered around our friend Lindsay with the task of helping to improve her backbend so she would no longer feel pain in it. After many group suggestions like "draw your tailbone back," "use a block between your thighs," "hug your elbows in," two peers pulled at ropes to support her hips and shoulders as she went into the pose. As she exclaimed, "Oh my god, I love you guys," I couldn't help but wonder if we could solve more of our classroom challenges this way. With shouts from a supportive community, who can see what we need to do, lovingly tell, instruct, and ultimately support us at our weak points to pull us out of pain and into a better place.

Thoughts on Classroom Management

80% of my classroom management is in having a relevant, rigorous, engaging curriculum and building relationships with students and community as a class. We create a community of purpose and belonging where each student knows that they are an important member of the class and that I am there to support them and their learning.

As an undergraduate at UC San Diego, I helped facilitate a weekly afterschool tutoring program for students who lived in a public housing project and attended elementary school in the affluent community of Del Mar, California. It was a small group of six students with a teacher supervising the room. One day he stepped out. Almost immediately, a third grader jumped out of his seat and started running around the room. Benito knew the teacher was the one who enforced boundaries and had authority, and now that he wasn't there, he was testing me. I failed miserably as he continued to run around the room ignoring my polite requests. And I learned so much that day about the importance of boundaries—kind boundaries—that are necessary for student learning.

Boundaries create safety. Students expect and need them. They take work and vigilance to set and maintain. They have a better chance of being honored if they are clearly communicated, fair, purposeful, enforced and reinforced equally for all, and built out of love and kindness. I tell students it's because I care that we are having this difficult conversation or that I am holding them to certain standards. It's because I have high expectations of them and that I care about them and their learning and the learning of our class that I'm willing to hold the line.

I've ranged through my career in how tightly I hold the boundaries and how tightly I hold the class—from drawing a hard line, to being more flexible, to negotiating expectations and boundaries. Each teacher develops their own style over time.

My second lesson from that afterschool program was on the importance of getting to know students. Fred was a second grader whose teachers were alarmed because out of all the people he could have chosen for his biography project, he chose Hitler. And so, as I was working with him one-on-one, I asked him about his project and why it was that he chose Hitler. He told me that he wanted to do it on Albert Einstein, but all the books about him were checked out. He had heard there was some sort of link between Einstein and Hitler. What an important lesson of leading with curiosity and nonjudgment and getting to know what students are interested in and what motivates them. For next session, I brought him a book on Einstein, which he then carried in his backpack every day thereafter.

The third lesson from that early time in education was the complexity of it all. Here were a group of students who were so bright and were attending a school with every resource available to them, but they were still behind their classmates in academic achievement. They largely stuck together with other students from the housing project rather than fully integrating into the school. Equity didn't just mean putting them in a good school so they can have equal resources. What it meant for them to get an education as students of color, with low socioeconomic status, and parents who may not have as much education or knowledge of how to navigate the system, was very different for their largely white and affluent counterparts. We could and should still maintain high expectations and standards for their success, but they would need additional supports in order to thrive and feel a sense of belonging in the classroom and school. How I engage all students and differentiate supports is essential to classroom management and student achievement.

As a teacher, I came to rely on the power of creating shared norms by asking each student, "What do you need so that you can learn in this class?" We make norms visible and return back to them. They communicate that each student is important here and we will do what we can to make sure each person can succeed here. Everyone is responsible and accountable for creating a community where the class can thrive. It is important to set the tone from the start. And to reset the tone when needed. They may test you, especially early on, and in those moments I have often leaned on kind boundaries with high expectations. There tend to be a few key students in a class. If you can identify them and get them on your side or give them a class leadership role, or align them to you, this can go a long way. Individual one-on-one conversations are helpful for building relationships and purpose to communicate expectations. A student may not be ready to walk in step with you when you are. Keep the window open for when that day is, and don't hold a grudge. They're just trying to make it in the world and it's not personal.

Before I began student teaching, my mentor, Heidi, told me about her class I would be taking on. With care, she went through each student in it and told me about who they were and what drove them. In that conversation, she was communicating to me that a class is made of the students in it. We are teaching people, not classes. And classroom management happens both at the individual and collective level.

Ultimately, my classroom management style landed on a combination of cultivating purpose and building community, grounded in meaningful curriculum and instruction and centered on the lives of students, communicating high, clear, and supported expectations, and caring about who my students are as people and what they need to thrive. They know I will protect them and our learning community and that they are important people in it. I know it sounds like a like a lot, but each one of these things is connected to the others. They are the drivers, not the extras. They are not separate from classroom management—they are it. All that work on the front end prevents me from having to do so much on the back end.

Assessment

How do we know if students have learned what we wanted them to learn? How do we measure and capture this and what do we do with that information? Assessments can be informal (check-in) or formal (quiz). They can be formative (checks along the way for understanding that uses this information to inform future learning) or summative (measures how much someone has learned). In designing assessments, multiple measures are ideal so that students have various ways of communicating their learning based on different learning modalities. Assessments may include a writing task, presentation, visual non-written (art or photography), Socratic discussion, exam, portfolio, etc.

Check for Understanding

Constantly checking for understanding ensures that all the students who started on the journey of the lesson, unit, semester, and class, are still in step by the end. It can be as simple and quick as a thumb up, sideways, or down to indicate whether they understand the skill or lesson or a reflection on what they learned.

Takeaways

Asking students reflective questions like "what are your take-aways?" or "what did you notice?" can help learning stick by involving them in an active learning process. This process of asking them to recall, make sense of, and synthesize their learning has been shown to help with retention and application of material. At the close of a lesson, I may ask them to share a takeaway with a partner, or we might do a quick lightning round of a one-word takeaway, or an exit slip where students write a takeaway of what they learned, what they thought of it, and a lingering question.

Rubrics

Rubrics help direct students toward goals and make it clear what is expected of them to earn a given score. They encourage and communicate high expectations. I recommend using a checklist rubric of criteria because it is usable, accessible and enables students to easily participate in the assessment process. I make rubrics visible and often will model a quality sample of student work for the class to show what they are aiming for.

To increase investment and understanding in my English class, students created their own class rubric. I asked them what makes "good" writing, then inserting their ideas into a structure that became the rubric. This helped them feel like part of the process and the rubric is our guide for examining writing and giving feedback. It is markedly easier to score the outputs (such as speaking and writing) than the inputs (such as listening and reading).

In creating a department writing rubric, our English team reviewed AP Literature, high school exit exam, and SAT exam rubrics. We then cross-listed them with the Common Core State Standards to look for commonalities across grade levels based on the components they all shared. Though each teacher varied the rubrics to some extent, it gave us access to the same language as we talked about writing across grade levels. Our writing rubric criteria:

- ◆ *Ideas*: depth and relevance (in critical thinking and responding to the prompt)
- ◆ *Evidence*: depth and relevance

- *Analysis*: depth and relevance
- *Style*: grammar, structure, spelling, vocabulary

It can be a useful experience for students to evaluate themselves and reflect on how they did. After our Introduction to Mindfulness group presentations, students reflect in their groups about their areas of strength and next steps based on the rubric criteria and submit a collective form of their reflections. Presentation rubric criteria:

- *Content*: clearly and concisely convey thoughtful ideas and examples
- *Application*: understanding and application of mindfulness principles
- *Voice*: volume, clarity, emotion, equity
- *Stance*: body language, eye contact, presence
- *Style*: effort, creativity, organization, applicability, interactivity, collaboration

Grading

I was told once that teaching was about managing two things: people and papers. The biggest advice I can give here is to make it sustainable and to place the most time and effort on the things that will make the biggest difference in student learning. For grading, there are four levels. No judgment—I have used them all.

Level 1: points only
Level 2: common comment for all (with verbal discussion as a class as to commonalities)
Level 3: common comment coupled with individual feedback
Level 4: individual feedback (verbal or written)

Feedback can help someone get from where they are to where they can go. So they know what to expect, I tell the class that I will give them an area of strength and a next step on feedback, and I also invite the discussion around what their relationship to feedback is. I try to be specific. Rather than "good job" I aim to give specific comments based on the rubric or their response.

Celebrate Success

Success is individual, group, and collective to the whole class and school. When success is broadened, students feel an increased sense of responsibility and pride. Do it early for an easy win to establish a culture of success and recognize milestones, whether the end of a project, week, unit, or semester, be it with clapping, high-fives, or even cake.

Classroom Application

A. Student activity: Create a KWL chart. List what you know about _____ topic, what you want to know, and (after the lesson) what you learned.

B. Student activity: Complete an exit ticket after the lesson that lists your takeaways, most interesting thing, and a question you might still have.

C. Create a shared rubric as a class.

Questions for Reflection or Discussion

1. For alignment, chart in three columns your goals, instructional methods, and assessment of a lesson, unit, or module.

Goals/Objectives	Instructional Methods	Assessment

2. What are ways you check for understanding and assess student learning?

3. What does classroom management mean to you? What lessons have you learned that have shaped your approach?

C. Application: Curriculum Design and Projects

Just like decorating a room, start with one interesting piece and build curriculum outward from there. It could be a text, question, or theme. I keep an ear to what students are interested in and what's happening in the world—sports, music, film, an interesting article or event—and try to incorporate these into the curriculum as a bridge to academic texts and content.

In creating curriculum, I start with the self and then go outwards from there—family, school, community, world. This situates students at the center of their learning and makes it accessible for them to participate. For example, our unit Here I Stand starts with the questions, "What do you believe in? What do you stand for?" And then we extend outwards to explore what others across literature and history believe in, how and why they stood for it in that way, and the effectiveness and outcomes of different methods.

I chunk a semester into units or modules and sequence these by starting small—both with texts (inputs) and assessments (outputs) and then building outwards. Summary of tips for planning fun and meaningful units:

1. *Themes*: explore themes that are relevant to student lives.
2. *Alignment*: align goals instruction, and assessment.
3. *Structure*: structure units with into, through, and beyond sequencing.
4. *Sequence*: start small and build up. Use short pieces as a hook to get students interested in the unit, then increase complexity and length. Excerpts are great for this.
5. *Component parts*: build upwards, breaking down component parts that are necessary to reaching a peak skill, culminating essay, or task.
6. *Touch points*: start inward and build out, then come back in. Start with individual lives of students, then expand outward to community, then country, then world, then relate back in.

7. *Questions*: use both questions for student self-reflection and also text reflection and analysis. I call them inquiry questions and critical questions. I take a lot of care in coming up with questions that will drive the curriculum and sustain interest.

8. *Bridge*: use accessible texts as bridges to traditional, more difficult or unfamiliar types of texts.

9. *Multiple genres*: mix it up by using multiple genres, including speeches, art, song, film, play, fiction, spoken word, history, news clips, magazine and newspaper articles, photographs, psychology experiments, research, policy, graphic novels, etc.

10. *Learning structures*: alternate learning structures between individual, pairs/small group, and whole group.

11. *Multiple learning modalities*: utilize visual, auditory, and kinesthetic learning styles. Create spaces for students who are artistic or have alternate strengths to shine.

12. *Project-based learning*: connect it all together with culminating projects that extend outside the classroom.

How content or assignments are introduced can spark interest and hook students into the curriculum. The smoother and clearer it is for students, the less confusion and more they can focus on learning. There is a learning curve or implementation dip when we try something new. Try to bring a growth mindset. Some tips I've found helpful for introducing a book or project to build investment and clarity:

1. *Purpose*: explain the purpose of *why* it is important and included in the course. What will students learn or gain from it? Why are they doing that project? Share about the topics the book will cover from the table of contents and explore why they might be important topics.

2. *Overview*: give an overview of *what* to expect. Go over the project details and schedule for book readings. Share about some features they might find interesting.

3. *Enthusiasm*: the more I'm excited as a teacher about what we're doing, the more students will be excited and invested. What's unique or special about it?
4. *Offer choices:* choosing their own book or project topic builds investment and relevance. This increases agency and personalized learning pathways.
5. *Clarity*: communicate what will be expected of them and by when. When should they have the book by and start reading? When should they begin their project and various components?
6. *Explore Together*: set aside time to explore topics for a project or skim the book to generate interest and momentum.
7. *Accountability*: tell them how their learning will be assessed. For a project, this can be by showing them the steps and rubric. For a book, perhaps mentioning that they will have points through the semester where they will need to bring in a quote, write reflections, or share about the book. So they know what to expect and encourage close reading, tell them upfront that there will be questions on the exam from the book that aren't covered in class. Assessments can be formal (presentation, exam), or also informal, such as asking them in class how their project is going, or what their takeaways from the book are so far. Mentioning course components repeatedly throughout the semester helps cue students to keep in step and stay on track.
8. *Questions*: invite space for students to ask questions. I prefer the wording "what questions do you have?" rather than "do you have any questions?"

Some of my favorite units over the years included themes of resilience and identity where students grappled with what it meant and took for them to thrive. Sample units are outlined here and included in-depth in Appendix A.

Unit 1: Here I Stand

- ◆ Essential Question: what does it mean to stand for something?
- ◆ Possible Core Texts: *Bhagavad Gita, Othello, Antigone, The Kite Runner, A Doll's House, The Apology, Between the World and Me, Invisible Women*
- ◆ Supplemental Texts: This I Believe; *The Best Advice I Ever Got*; speech "Perils of Indifference," Elie Wiesel; short story "The Country of the Blind," H.G. Wells; *Borderlands*, Gloria Anzaldua; Prometheus myth
- ◆ Art: *Guernica*, Picasso; *Icarus*, Matisse
- ◆ Song: "Where is the Love?," Black-Eyed Peas
- ◆ Film: *Promising Young Woman*
- ◆ Historical Connections: educational equity, civil rights movement, environment
- ◆ Culminating Essay: using at least three of the texts studied in this unit, analyze the causes, methods, and results of choosing something to stand for. Include what the individuals stand for, why they make the decisions they do, what factors enable their success or failure, and discuss the broader implications of their actions.
- ◆ Project: create a written statement and visual representation of what you stand for and the challenges that you've overcome to get to where you are. Present in a class showcase.

Unit 2: Times of Transition

- ◆ Essential Questions: what are the elements of a transition? What makes a transition successful or unsuccessful? According to what criteria? What is the importance, benefit, and/or danger, of transitions? How can transitions be leveraged/optimized for greatest positive growth?
- ◆ Possible Core Texts: *One Flew Over the Cuckoo's Nest, The Piano Lesson, Hamlet, A Place for Us, The Sweetness of Water, How to be an Antiracist*

- Supplemental Texts: *A Taste of Power, Tipping Point, Pygmalion*
- Art: Jackson Pollack, Andy Warhol, Banksy
- Song: student choice
- Film: *Antwone Fisher*
- Historical Connection: transitions in cities and communities, technology and globalization
- Culminating Essay: choose three of the individuals studied to determine who had the strongest transition. Include in your response the elements of a successful transition, the factors that made that individual more successful in the transition than the others, and the implications of the transition.
- Projects: A. write and illustrate a children's book about a transition. B. Create a map of transitions faced in your life, family, and community. Include what it took to make it through the transitions.

Unit 3: The Quest

- Essential Questions: what does it mean to be on a quest for something? What are the challenges and opportunities of a quest? How can a quest be optimized for greater chances of fulfillment?
- Possible Core Texts: *The Alchemist, Into the Wild, The Stranger, Candide, Angels in America, A Raisin in the Sun, The Odyssey, Siddhartha, Know My Name, The Vanishing Half, Educated, My Grandmother's Hands*
- Supplemental Texts: Road Poems: "The Road Not Taken," Robert Frost; "Shoulders," Naomi Shihab Nye; "Uphill," Christina Rossetti. Other poems: "Love Song of J. Alfred Prufrock," T.S. Eliot; "Howl," Allen Ginsberg, Short stories: "I Stand Here Ironing," Tillie Olsen "The Garden of Forking Paths", Jorge Luis Borges. Book excerpt: *Blink*, Malcolm Gladwell
- Visual: advertisements
- Song: "Lose Yourself," Eminem
- Film: *Slumdog Millionaire*
- Historical Connection: technology and industrialization

◆ Culminating Essay: using at least three of the sources studied this unit, analyze the elements of a successful quest. Discuss how and why the characters went in search of their goals as well as why their quests resulted as they did.

◆ Project: Create a quest guidebook or boardgame that includes your philosophy of being on a quest.

Other identity and resilience themed units I've loved creating and teaching include:

◆ *How to Make it in America*, where students explore what success is for them and what it takes and costs to be successful.

◆ *Where I'm At, Where I'm From, Where I'm Going*, where students explore their own identities alongside the identities of individuals in history and literature.

◆ *Decision Making in Times of Crisis*, exploring the decisions before, during, and after a time of difficulty that contributes to the outcome. There inevitably is one that arises in the world when we are in this unit.

Curricular Projects

Some of my favorite projects over the years include:

1. Each student writes a poem (or story or favorite recipe). We compile each submission into a class book. Artistic students design the cover art. This is a simple way of creating class community and honoring each student's voice.

2. *Antigone* Rock Musical. I had a class with student musicians who loved music and when we got to the part of the chorus in *Antigone*, they asked if they were supposed to sing it. I jokingly said yes, but it stuck. And after we finished reading the play, students brought in instruments and we recreated it as a musical.

3. Children's books where students write and illustrate their own children's books, which can be based on a studied topic, theme, or book.

4. A magazine or newspaper where students write articles from the perspective of people from a time period, philosophy, or book.

5. Community exhibition of student art and or stories. Sharing student work with a larger community builds investment and pride, and includes families and communities in student learning.

6. Guest speakers. Inviting others to speak about their careers, work, or topics studied exposes students to role models and multiple perspectives.

7. Invite mock judges to evaluate student presentations and give feedback to students for real-world assessments.

8. Ted Talks where students share their philosophies on what it takes to make it in America. They can also give the talk from the perspective of a person in history or literature.

9. NPR StoryCorps interviews where students interview someone. They can also assume the roles of a person in history or literature.

10. Mental Health Research and Video Project where students pick a topic in mental health, develop a research question around it, write a paper, and create a video PSA to share about their topic. Sample student research questions include: "How does bullying affect the mental health of teens?" and "What is the relationship between teenage depression and social interaction? What can teenagers do to overcome their own depression?" Project details included in Appendix A.

11. Spring Forum on Education. Similarly, students pick a topic in education, develop a research question, write a paper, and then present in a forum with invited guests. Sample student research questions include: "What type of personality is more successful in a classroom environment?" and "Why do some students fail and some pass in the same class?"

12. Gallery exhibition and presentation of student art and artist statements. I've done this both at a local art gallery

and at a café where we invited families and showcased student work.

13. Student blog where students post about a topic, and then a colleague's students responded in a dialogue across classrooms.

14. My grandest project was The Learner Project, where students explored the essential question "What does it mean to be a learner?" They wrote learner statements, studied education policy in their history class, interviewed others about their educational journeys, created artwork on the topic in their art classes, and showcased their art in a presentation and exhibition at the U.S. Department of Education. One student, Maria, who later graduated from Mills College, reflected about the experience, "This trip allowed us the opportunity to share our opinions and lend our voices to the very same people who can make changes. We learned that anyone with eyes and ears can find a problem, but it takes critical thinking to come up with solutions." She reflected that they grew essential skills of public speaking, problem solving, teamwork, and work ethic. "Our voices were not only heard by adults at the heart of our education system, but they were fully valued and validated." Sample learner statements and artwork are included in Appendix B.

It doesn't have to be a fancy or involved project. Giving students an opportunity to reflect on who they are and what it means for them personally to be in the classroom or learning that subject area can go a long way in building purpose, investment, and academic skills.

Classroom Application

A. Student activity: Bring in a song, poem, or story related to a selected theme.
B. Ask students: What does it mean for you to be a learner?
C. Create a class book where everyone contributes a poem, recipe, or story.

Questions for Reflection or Discussion

1. Looking back on your schooling, what have been your most memorable projects?

2. What does an engaging and purposeful curriculum mean or look like to you?

3. What is the most exciting and the most unpleasant/ daunting thing about curriculum design to you?

4. What parts of a curriculum do you think are most or least interesting for your students?

Bibliography

Armstrong, P. (2010). Bloom's Taxonomy. Vanderbilt University Center for Teaching. Retrieved from https://cft.vanderbilt.edu/guides-sub-pages/blooms-taxonomy/

Aungst, G. (2014, September 4). Categorizing tasks according to the complexity of thought they require is one way for teachers to create a rich learning environment. *Edutopia.* Retrieved from https://www.edutopia.org/blog/webbs-depth-knowledge-increase-rigor-gerald-aungst

Baumeister, R., & Tierney, J. (2011). *Willpower: Rediscovering the greatest human strength.* New York: Penguin.

Bronk, K.C. (2017, December 21). Five Ways to Foster Purpose in Adolescents. *Greater Good Magazine.* Retrieved from https://greatergood.berkeley.edu/article/item/five_ways_to_foster_purpose_in_adolescents

California Global Education Project. Global Competence Framework. Retrieved from http://calglobaled.org/global-competence

Chaiklin, S. (2003). "The Zone of Proximal Development in Vygotsky's analysis of learning and instruction." In Kozulin, A., Gindis, B., Ageyev, V. & Miller, S. (Eds.) *Vygotsky's educational theory and practice in cultural context.* 39–64. Cambridge: Cambridge University. https://doi.org/10.1017/CBO9780511840975.004

Duhigg, C. (2012). *The power of habit: Why we do what we do in life and business.* New York: Random House.

Dweck, C.S. (2008). *Mindset: The new psychology of success.* New York: Ballantine Books.

Elliot, A. J., & Church, M. A. (1997). A hierarchical model of approach and avoidance achievement motivation. *Journal of Personality and Social Psychology, 72*(1), 218–232. https://doi.org/10.1037/0022-3514.72.1.218

Hill, P. L., & Turiano, N. A. (2014). Purpose in life as a predictor of mortality across adulthood. *Psychological Science, 25*(7), 1482–1486. https://doi.org/10.1177/0956797614531799

Kim, E. S., Kawachi, I., Chen, Y., & Kubzansky, L. D. (2017). Association Between Purpose in Life and Objective Measures of Physical Function in Older Adults. *JAMA psychiatry, 74*(10), 1039–1045. https://doi.org/10.1001/jamapsychiatry.2017.2145

Into-Through-Beyond: 2020. a lesson-planning framework for using YES! in the classroom. *Yes! Magazine*. Retrieved from https://www.yesmagazine.org/education/2004/08/08/into-through-beyond-a-lesson-planning-framework-for-using-yes-in-the-classroom

KWL Charts. 2020. *Facing History*. Retrieved from https://www.facinghistory.org/resource-library/teaching-strategies/k-w-l-charts

Locke, E. A., & Latham, G. P. (2002). Building a practically useful theory of goal setting and task motivation: A 35-year odyssey. *American Psychologist*, *57*(9), 705–717. https://doi.org/10.1037/0003-066X.57.9.705

PISA 2018 Global Competence. Retrieved from https://www.oecd.org/pisa/innovation/global-competence/

Tatum, B.D. (1997) *"Why Are All the Black Kids Sitting Together in the Cafeteria?" and Other Conversations About Race*. New York: Basic Books.

Theobald, E. J., Hill, M. J., Tran, E., Agrawal, S., Arroyo, E. N., Behling, S., Chambwe, N., Cintrón, D. L., Cooper, J. D., Dunster, G., Grummer, J. A., Hennessey, K., Hsiao, J., Iranon, N., Jones, L., 2nd, Jordt, H., Keller, M., Lacey, M. E., Littlefield, C. E., Lowe, A., … Freeman, S. (2020). Active learning narrows achievement gaps for underrepresented students in undergraduate science, technology, engineering, and math. *Proceedings of the National Academy of Sciences of the United States of America*, *117*(12), 6476–6483. https://doi.org/10.1073/pnas.1916903117

What is PBL? Buck Institute for Education. Retrieved from https://www.pblworks.org/what-is-pbl

Wiggins, G., & McTighe, J. (2005). *Understanding by Design*. 2nd ed. Upper Saddle River, NJ: Pearson.

2

Foundation 2: Investment

Why should I care?

FIGURE 2.1

DOI: 10.4324/9781003318408-2

A. Relationships

When I first started teaching, I was told that they don't care what you know until they know that you care. That we can't just like our students, we have to love our students. And to ask, "what if it was my child?" Because they are all our children. This might feel like a tall task when all we signed up for was to teach our subject areas, but building relationships is what has enabled me to be able to teach content on such a deep level and keep students in step with me. Students need to know not only why they are doing what they are doing, and that what they put in is worth what they will get out, but also that the person asking them to do it cares about them doing it. Charlotte Danielson wrote, "Teaching depends, fundamentally, on the quality of the relationships among individuals." The relationships we have with our students enable learning to take place and create a safe and caring environment where students can take risks, put in effort toward a goal, and work with others to transcend boundaries.

Through my career, I've vacillated in what this means. I started teaching in my early twenties, and I think in the beginning was seen in more of a big sister role. Along the way, it became clearer what it meant to care for my students and I what I had to do and be so that they could maximally learn in my classroom. Boundaries were necessary for learning and didn't mean that I didn't care—conversely, they meant that I cared enough to set and maintain them. I probably steered a little too firmly initially after being too loose, and then found a balance I was comfortable with between deeply caring for them personally, while setting kind boundaries to enable their learning.

The stronger the personal and group relationships in the classroom, the more students will allow a teacher to teach them. It is not to say that a strong relationship equates to a rigorous, differentiated, relevant curriculum, but that it is the foundation upon which everything else is built. We teach people, not subject areas. Building relationships with students helps create trust, investment, and a culture of caring in the classroom where every student feels as though they matter. When students feel seen, heard, and understood, they know that they are important and what they have to say is important.

In a research study, participants observed that a hill didn't seem as steep if they had a friend alongside them, or even thought of a friend. This is true in life too—that our challenges are easier to bear when we have others alongside us. Relationships are a protective factor that can create the conditions for resilience and learning in the classroom.

Relationships occur on multiple levels in a classroom: teacher to student, teacher to class, student to student, students to students, and student to class. Structured opportunities for pair and small group discussion builds trust among classmates. It starts with knowing names. Asking how students are doing. Wanting to know who they are and what is important to them. Relationships allow for the safety and trust required for learning to occur. I found this to be especially important the more guarded students were and the more vulnerable the work was that we were doing. Students who were hardened by the education system and resistant to learning needed to know that I cared about them and that they were important in our classroom. As we explored their inner stories, hopes, fears, and patterns, students needed to know that what they shared would be held with care by me and their classmates. This is the prerequisite for being able to learn in a way that challenges students to step out of their comfort zone and participate in the deep discussions about what it means to be human and resilient in the midst of challenges.

How is that caring communicated in the classroom? Gary Chapman's Five Love Languages describes ways that caring can be communicated and received. This can be translated into the classroom in intentional ways:

1. *Physical touch*: when appropriate, a high-five or pat on the shoulder.
2. *Verbal affirmation*: specific praise for a good job on student performance.

3. *Quality time*: equitably giving time and attention to students.
4. *Acts of service*: organizing a fieldtrip or helping a student in need.
5. *Gifts*: an appropriate gift given to all students, such as a personalized bookmark or cookies.

Student Stories and Identity

I tell students that of all the stories we read, there is none more powerful or important than their own. Each year since I started teaching, no matter the subject, students write and share their own resilience stories. They reflect on what made them who they are today, the moments that changed their lives, and the people they are on their way to becoming. Below is an excerpt of a personal narrative from my former student, Miguel.

> "Ey foo, where you from?" Five simple words that if asked to me two years ago could have gotten me put in the hospital or running from the police. Five words that I heard on a daily basis, and the days that I wouldn't hear them, were actually weird to me. "Ey foo, where you from?" I guess to me those words were an invitation to start something, to show whoever asked what I, as a soldier, represented, what I stood for. What can I say … I was a young kid, and I didn't quite realize the things I was getting myself into. I didn't realize the consequences of my actions at that point in my life. I thought that the gang life was something to be proud of, something to admire, and something to be a part of. Now I know that I was wrong. People often say, "you learn from your own mistakes, not anyone else's." And I am living proof of that saying. This is my story …

Student stories create community and make the life of the learner central to learning. They have helped me to understand where students are coming from and the scars and hearts they carry.

Tips on sharing stories in the classroom:

- ◆ Set the expectation that everyone shares, including the teacher. I tell them they don't have to share anything they're not comfortable sharing, and at the same time there is a power in owning their story and speaking it.
- ◆ Have students interview each other, family, or community members for their stories.
- ◆ Create a safe space by affirming that whatever is said in the room stays in the room. I tell them upfront that the only exception to this is that because teachers are mandated reporters, if a student is in danger, I would have to report it.
- ◆ Explore compiling student stories into a class book if everyone is comfortable.

Sharing stories can also transcend stereotypes and break down boundaries. After students share their stories, I also always share one. My Junior American Literature class one year started with the question "What does it mean to be _____ in America?" I knew from the first day of school that Ali was Palestinian, as that was his group identification he wrote about. I am Israeli American. The last project of the school year ended with students telling their personal American story. Ali told his about discrimination after 9/11. I told a story of anti-Semitism I faced as a college student. Afterwards he wrote a note to me, "You have changed my life by telling me your story. I don't know why, but I felt like if you were my sister when you said your narrative. I used to be like I won't talk to or associate myself with any Israeli, but you changed that all. ... We're all brothers and sisters in this world. Peace." Shared stories connect us all and students often remark that hearing the stories of others makes them feel not so alone in theirs.

Trust

Trust takes effort to build and is easy to lose. The more students trust a teacher, the more they will invest in themselves as learners in the class. Every interaction is an opportunity to build and strengthen trust. Tips include:

1. Know student names, interests, and identities
2. Follow up and follow through
3. Be clear, fair, and consistent
4. Tell them the reasons for decisions and share decision-making when possible
5. Never hold a grudge
6. Keep the window open for whenever a student is ready
7. Trust them and show them that they are trusted
8. Build reputation
9. Treat them like people
10. Keep expectations high, clear, and supported

Classrooms can be structured to create spaces to build trust. Having a third space to talk about another topic can lead to more personal conversations. One way I did this as a high school teacher was to hold individual meetings as the class worked on something that didn't require my attention. These sessions lasted 5–10 minutes and generally contained four questions:

1. How is your notebook going?
2. How are your skills improving?
3. How are things going for you otherwise?
4. How is _____ (something specific I know about that individual student) going?

The initial focus on the notebook allows us to then extend the conversation in a safe, structured way and create a space for students to speak about things going on in their lives.

Teaching in a university, the space for this conversation is different, and I try to check in with each student before or after class, with a simple "how are you doing?" or following up on something I know about with "how is _____ going?" When students enter my classroom, just as if they were entering my home, I greet them by name and ask them how they are. One student reflected in a course evaluation that this simple greeting "makes me feel so happy and cared for." Each moment with a student is an opportunity to check in and communicate caring. Creating a culture of caring and trust where everyone feels safe and supported is not only a powerful practice in and of itself, but it's a vehicle for student learning and enables students to feel comfortable to participate and open up and take risks. Another student wrote in an evaluation of my mindfulness course, "This was one of the few classes that I actually felt close to my classmates… (it was) such a warm, inviting and non-judgmental space where we could all be ourselves and share things without worrying." Another noticed, "I always felt comfortable talking in this class, which is different for me as I am a very shy student." A safe classroom space enables learning to occur as students step outside their comfort zones and lower their guards. It starts with communicating caring to students and making sure they feel seen and know that they are important to the classroom community.

When trust is broken, it is important to take authentic steps to repair it soon after. This can begin with individually checking in with a student and asking, "is everything ok?" or asking how they are feeling. Share your perspective or why you made the choice you made. Communicate caring and let them know that your relationship with them is important to you and that they are important to you. Say what you hope will happen in the future. Follow up and follow through on any next steps.

Classroom Application

A. When possible, greet each student individually by name as they come into class and ask how they are doing.
B. Ask students to write and share their personal narrative of what made them into who they are today.
C. Student activity: Interview a fellow student to learn their story and what shaped them into who they are. Write their story, create a visual of them, or share with the class what you learned about who they are. This can also be done across classrooms or grade levels.

Questions for Reflection or Discussion

1. What are the ways students know they are cared about in the/your classroom? What does it take to create a safe and comfortable classroom community?

2. Which students do you have the most positive relationships with? Why?

3. What are the times when you've felt you've gained or lost trust in the classroom?

B. Ownership

When we own something, we are more inclined to value it and take care of it. Ownership helps students invest in the classroom and the work they are doing in it. Giving them responsibility communicates trust and tells them that they are important. I tell them it is *their* classroom, *our* classroom, not *my* classroom. In the later years of my high school teaching, each student had a class job they chose from a list that included roles like the breathing leader, who helped us all take a few breaths to start class, the receptionist who answered the phone, the librarian who managed our classroom library, and the paper passer who made sure students all had the papers they needed. Each job was important to running a smooth classroom and allowed me to focus on teaching. It gave them a sense of pride and ownership over a part of our classroom. Students took responsibility and learned skills within their jobs. On her own, the breathing leader took the time to download a meditation app and learn about word choices that could be helpful for meditations. The bell ringer looked up videos on how to create a smooth vibration with the singing bowl to start class. The receptionist was so eager to do her job, she ran to the phone each time it rang. Students thought of new creative ways to do their job and had a specific role that helped our classroom function.

In my college mindfulness classroom, where the phone doesn't ring and there are no papers to pass, there is the expectation of a collective job as contributing, active students in the classroom. We sit in a circle and every session they share in small group and whole group discussion. Ownership is also created through choice and trust. Students choose how many minutes per day they will meditate and communicate that number to the class so there is shared responsibility and accountability. For the group project, they choose an area of daily life to bring mindfulness to, whether technology, eating, self-care, communication, or decision-making. I tell them to make it meaningful for them and to pick a strategy that will be useful for their lives. For both meditation and their group strategies, I tell them that I won't be there with them in their living room to be sure they do it. It's on them. And at the same time, what would be the point of being in the class if they weren't going to invest in themselves? I encourage them to think of what would happen and how might it enhance their lives if they did invest the time and effort.

Student Leadership

When a high school I taught in didn't have funding for a college counselor, I created a Peer College Leadership course where students were tasked with building a college-going culture. I told them that now we have 26 college counselors. I said I didn't know how we were going to do it, but we were. And with the stakes so high, we had to. Peer College Leaders (PCLs) broadened their perspective on education and were themselves transformed by the role. They learned tangible skills through a shared purpose of educational empowerment. Alongside creating a visible college culture, meeting individually with students across grade levels, and presenting in classrooms, family workshops, and to district administrators, students found that it was they themselves who were most changed by the process. One student reflected, "The experience as a PCL has motivated me to be someone in life to pass down the knowledge I have gained and what I will gain in the future. The experience has impacted me to pursue a career—a dream that will help others in my community." Another observed, "Being in this class has helped me explore my ability to become someone greater. I would not have believed myself to be a leader or any type of teacher for our students." He found it changed his perspective of what they are all capable of. "The job of teaching others about college made me more responsible and matured my way of thinking."

Students were given meaningful opportunities to contribute that helped them know that they are important. In their acts of service, they became more invested in our classroom and school as they were themselves changed by the experience. A student who went on to earn a master's degree in counseling reflected that as a PCL he "became aware of the individual and collective power our class had in promoting a college-going culture."

The experience motivated him toward a career where he could help others. "I knew that as an advisor, teacher, and mentor I could be an important resource for students and their families and foster personal, academic, and career growth."

We can start to shift norms through aligning goals, dialogue, and activities while investing students in the process. Here are some ways we helped shift the norm toward a greater college-going culture:

1. Invite former students to regularly speak to current students about their experience. The smaller the ratio of students to speaker, the greater the impact.
2. Increase exposure through college visits or fieldtrips to performances that take place on college campuses to help students visualize themselves there in the future.
3. Invite college and career representatives to speak in classrooms.
4. Increase visibility through posting college information, acceptances, motivational quotes, and wearing college shirts.
5. Dialogue about success and refocus students on goals so that they internalize high expectations and consider that success is possible to achieve.
6. Community Career Days, where professionals from the community speak about their careers. This helps students connect with people who used education as a pathway to their success.
7. Career preparation that may include career exploration, resume building, and mock interviews.
8. Use curricular examples of individuals striving for success to examine success-inducing skills of resilience and goal setting. Explore what might get in the way of success and how to mitigate these factors.
9. Get "key" students. There are usually a few key students in class who can help shift norms. Building relationships with them is crucial.
10. Encourage students to apply for internships or work with others to start a school-community internship program.

A year after she competed my university mindfulness course, I received an email from a student asking for my help starting a mindfulness course in her community in India. She told me, "The suicide rate in India is rising alarmingly fast, and unfortunately, so many of those are young people who're unable to deal with the overwhelming situations they're facing in their lives." In the prior month, seven teenagers in her small city took their own lives. "I've decided to do something and try to help as many students as possible. I want to introduce mindfulness to schools here and try to break the stigma around mental health." She felt empowered to take action in her community with the skills she built. "After taking your class, I have genuinely felt so confident in my skill to take care of my own mental well-being. I always feel like I have the tools and strategies I need to help me in overwhelming/challenging situations." She never before thought a class would have such a meaningful impact on her life. "Now I would like to spread this knowledge to others too."

Motivation

Dan Pink's book *Drive* highlights three intrinsic motivators of performance: autonomy, mastery, and purpose. Student motivation can increase when they are given a choice of what they are learning, the tools for skill development, and when they know that what they are doing has a meaningful purpose. Conversely, while it may seem to work in the short term, extrinsic motivation of performing a task because of an external reward is found to be not as sustainable or effective.

When students make a structured choice within an assignment, they are not just choosing a topic, they are making the choice to say they will learn and do something. With their choice, they are opting into the task. This could be in the form of a choice of pre-selected prompts, choosing from a list of topics, or determining their own area of exploration. For our Mental Health Research Project, I gave students the umbrella of mental health, and we explored various components of it within the classroom. They then chose which mental health topic they wanted to explore and developed an individual research question around that area. This ownership of choice and topic situates them as the expert in what they're learning. When they share that knowledge with others in structured discussions and presentations, they then possess a certain knowledge base that they can bring and own. Their interest drives ownership, and ownership further develops interest. As young adults are developing more independence, giving them a choice within a structured assignment can be a motivator to learn and contribute their unique perspective and knowledge to the class. They learn that what they have to say is important and that they are an important part of class learning. Learning then doesn't only become something the teacher gives to the student, but a dynamic process of discovery that students actively participate in.

Purpose is continually messaged in my classroom through coming back to why what we are doing is important. We start in the *why*. From there, we look at *how* we build skills, and *what* content and activities we use to build it. The content is a vehicle for student learning and growth. It is secondary to the skills, knowledge, and dispositions that students develop along the way. Investment gives students a reason to be open to learning.

Supporting high expectations in the classroom can make a rigorous curriculum accessible and possible. It can help students achieve their highest potential of learning. Belen reflected, "if it weren't for the extra attention my teachers gave me, I wouldn't have built the self-confidence or skills that have allowed me to succeed in school." Growing up in a single parent, immigrant home, she didn't feel as though her mom understood the extent of her accomplishments, and she turned to teachers for support. She remembers the impact of her fourth grade teacher, Mr. Goodell, who saw her potential. "My teachers had high expectations for me and made me want to live up to them." This shaped her work ethic and helped her feel as though they were looking out for her. "Knowing that they were watching me made me feel as though they cared about my education, cared about me as a person, and were expecting me to succeed. Luckily, this teacher was just one of the first to challenge me in this way and made me feel that extra ounce of 'special' that led me to believe that I couldn't let my teachers down." High and supported expectations can set the bar for students to reach for, and give them the tools to get there.

Owning Success

Students need to know that they can be successful in a class and that it is possible for them. They need to know this early and feel as though they have something to lose if they give up. I like to start with a small, easy, early win. Some tips include:

- ◆ *Make it Possible*. Students need to know that they can do what a teacher is asking them to do. They need to believe that they can do it. The more students feel like they have the tools to thrive in a class where the teacher cares about their learning, the more they will be invested in the class and succeed.
- ◆ *Value*. Students need to know that what they put in is worth what they will get out. They need to know that if they are taking a risk in the classroom and going to invest time, energy, and possibly their identities, then it better be worth something to them.
- ◆ *Alignment*. Aligning with student goals and interests can help students see a teacher as someone they can trust to help them thrive. Choose battles wisely and strategically for alignment and credibility. Avoid going to battle, but if you do, make sure you win.
- ◆ *Share and celebrate successes*. Notice when students do something well. Praise them, celebrate successes and make success visible and possible. They want to be successful. As teachers we can create the conditions, expectations, and support to make it easier for them to be.

Student-Centered Classrooms

A student-centered classroom builds on student interests and styles. It places them at the center of their learning. This enables the teaching of rigorous skills with high, clear, and supported expectations geared toward student strengths, styles, ways of interacting, culture, and relevance. Building ownership through choice, commitment, and interest directly increases investment. When students experience shared decision-making power, they are more invested in their success.

In a teacher-centered classroom, the teacher is the source of knowledge and presents information to students who are expected to retain it. In a student-centered classroom, learning is dynamically created through interaction with content and activities. The teacher becomes more of a facilitator or coach and students have agency to play an active role in their learning. I tell students that their learning doesn't start or stop depending on whether or not I'm standing in front of them. Some of my proudest teacher moments happened when I wasn't even there: a note from a substitute on how impressed she was that a student ran the class while I was away, or in an online class, when my Zoom connection cut out and with graduation around the corner, I returned to find a student reading aloud to the rest the Dr. Seuss book *Oh the Places You'll Go*. These moments reflect the pride and ownership students take in the class. The class is more than me and they took initiative to play an active role in our class community.

Alongside this, a relevant curriculum infused with student culture increases the investment, engagement, and value they place on the class. It is not a choice between rigorous or engaging material to teach. A relevant, student-centered curriculum is about taking material and relating the themes, content, and stories of the human condition to student lives. Engagement is not an end—it is a vehicle to deepen student learning. Matching traditional texts with modern texts can help bridge student and school culture. For example, in my early years teaching, when I needed a text to go with T.S. Eliot's poem "The Love Song of J. Alfred Prufrock," I asked students if they had any ideas for a song about someone who either strives to achieve what they want or isn't able to. My student, Juan, suggested Eminem's "Lose Yourself," which turned out to be a powerful contrast. Investment increased by involving them in the learning process. This shows value for the knowledge they come into the class with and can hook them into learning.

Classroom Application

A. Ask students to sign up for a class job.
B. Include multiple prompts in a task for students to choose between.
C. Invite a former student to speak about their experience in college or their career.

Questions for Reflection or Discussion

1. What motivates you? What do you think motivates your students?

2. When do students seem to feel most successful in your classroom?

3. What does a student-centered classroom mean and look like to you?

C. Application: Community Partnerships

A colleague and friend, Nancy, recently asked me if I am still able to have the same kind of community involvement in my university classes as I did as a high school teacher. The answer is that it's different, and I'm still trying to figure out what it authentically looks like.

As a high school teacher, I sought to blur the lines between classroom and community and bring the outside in and take my students out in the real world. Whether through guest speakers, fieldtrips, events in the community, or partnerships with organizations, the more real-world exposure students got, the more invested and interested they were.

One semester I had a particularly active and difficult ninth grade class of mostly males right before lunchtime. My solution was to turn to community supports and flood them with male role models of color who could reach them in a way I hadn't been able to. I incorporated arts education to channel their powerful voices. They participated in the August Wilson In-School Residency Program, where an actor from the program, Tony, came in weekly to teach them about the plays of August Wilson through performance. On Fridays, a poet from the Say Word poetry program came in to teach them about poetry and worked with them to create a class poetry book. Based on the August Wilson Monologue Competition that the Music Center hosted, we planned our own classroom event where students chose and recited August Wilson monologues. We read the play *Fences* as a class and went on a fieldtrip to see a performance of an August Wilson play. Students were invited to see the official Monologue Competition at the Music Center with their parents. In this class that was very vocal and animated and always bordered on chaos, the times we could just channel that chaos into learning, those would be my favorite teaching moments of the day. David Cohen's book *Capturing the Spark* recounts a day he visited that class when students were performing an unrehearsed reading of a scene from the play *Fences*:

> Two boys improvise a gesture portraying their shared grief: facing each other with hands on the other's shoulders, they bow their heads until their foreheads touch, and they pause for a moment. As the emotional tone of the scene shifts, one young man exclaims, "I don't want to be Troy Maxwell, I wanna be *me!*"—punctuated with three loud slaps to his chest. Then there's a part of the script that requires singing a song—something about the family dog—and the boy reading the part is game, trying to improvise a little melody to accompany the words. His peers in the audience provide a beat, and he begins singing something closer to the blues, but he then changes the tune again, turning the text into a rap.

This class that was my most difficult, with community partnership, a relevant curriculum, role models, and space for student voices was transformed. Students found relevance, inserted themselves and their voices, style, and culture into the play. It was a dynamic process where students brought a text to life through community engagement and saw themselves reflected in their learning. Cohen writes that "it's the confluence of Linda's broader vision, Tony's charisma and talent, and the depth and emotion of August Wilson's writing that have combined to bring out excellent work in these students."

As difficult as that semester was, at the end of it, my students were asking me if I taught tenth grade too. Sure, all that took work to organize, and perhaps I could have ultimately found a way to reach them on my own, but that would also be work, and not as fun for either of us if we kept slogging along. The community was the answer here, as was getting key students to invest in what we're doing and see themselves reflected in the curriculum and those who came into our classroom. Community partnership wasn't separate from the curriculum—it was the curriculum, and was tailored to fit student needs, interests, and identities.

Meanwhile in a curricular unit on identity, my sophomore English class partnered with The Getty Center and community organization 826LA for an exhibition on student identity and self-portraiture. Students toured the museum with Japanese photographer Tomoko Sawada, who had an exhibition there on her self-portraits. Back in the classroom, students met with community volunteers to design and refine their own self-portraits and artist statements, and ultimately hosted an art exhibition at a coffee shop in the community for families and others to view their work. Students named the exhibit Identity 37, to account for the importance of each of the 37 individuals who were part of our class and the exhibition. One student, Gabe, who portrayed his self-portrait as a staircase he climbed, wrote in his artist statement:

> At some point, we all are faced with a challenge. A problem that has to be overcome in some shape or form. Much like a staircase, these small challenges can come one after another; the next one is usually higher in importance than the one before it. After reaching the top of the staircase, one may experience relief or exhilaration from the effort given to ascend the slope. The same feelings occur when one succeeds during their life, especially after a long journey up the stairway that everyone attempts to ascend: success. The end result is uncertain, oftentimes slightly blurred and hazy. Even previous challenges may become forgotten after the climb becomes longer and the end nears. Many others climb this same stairway, myself included…

For the exhibition, a group of three students took initiative to ask if they could sing Ed Sheeran's song "Photograph." Of the experience, a student reflected, "It inspired me to work hard so that I can have a great future. It impacted me by finding my inner self and focusing on what doors to open for my future." Another observed, "It helped me find and understand my identity. The experience helped me look deeper inside myself and be vulnerable enough to let myself and others in to help me figure it out.

It impacted me to be open with myself." Community partnership in project-based learning was not separate from the curriculum—it was a vehicle for student voice and accessing the curriculum.

It doesn't have to be fancy, or even well-thought out. It can be an organic process that arises with the needs, circumstances, and resources available. A student in that sophomore class had a parent whose job others thought was cool, and so I invited him in for a Career Talk, which then became a regular occurrence for various parents to be guest speakers in the class. We needed extra chaperones for a fieldtrip, and parents volunteered. Each class is different, and it takes keeping and ear to what it is that students are interested in, what resources are available, and how to incorporate them into the curriculum.

Bridging communities and schools involves coordination on top of the already full plates of teachers and community organizations. It isn't that it's necessarily more work—it's different work, and work that is an investment in students and the curriculum. Bridging classrooms and communities involves bringing the outside world into the classroom and bringing the classroom into the outside world, blurring the lines between school and community. This can be done though guest speakers, fieldtrips, community-based projects, a class blog, or countless other ways to involve students in meaningful experiences that extend the classroom walls. Tips for bridging classrooms and communities:

- ◆ Brainstorm classroom and community needs and identify local community organizations who align with them.
- ◆ Reach out to organizations. Discuss a current class project that might be enriched with a guest speaker or fieldtrip. Brainstorm together how to address a school or community need.
- ◆ Invite guest speakers from various careers, colleges, or organizations. Plan a school Career Day and invite speakers from various fields to speak about their careers.
- ◆ Invite former students or alumni in colleges or careers to speak about their experiences.

- ◆ Invite experts from the field to help students with projects, like a local artist to help with an upcoming art project.
- ◆ Plan student projects or presentations with invited guests in the audience or to judge student work.
- ◆ Partner with a community organization to host project presentations at their organization.
- ◆ Plan or participate in a community event, such as a 5k, where schools, families, community organizations, and businesses are engaged in a common goal.
- ◆ Write letters to an elected official, magazine, newspaper, or author.
- ◆ Plan projects with teachers in other classrooms, schools, states, or countries, including a shared unit, blog, Zoom, or pen pal exchange.
- ◆ Invite students to interview individuals in their families and communities.
- ◆ Invite students to submit online entries to a website or comment on a blog.
- ◆ Maintain a good relationship with community speakers for future projects and opportunities to connect.

As a university educator, it's different. I've invited dozens of guest speakers to speak in my classroom to share their perspectives, and though this has been impactful, it isn't the same as sustained project-based partnerships. I mostly feel like I'm on the other side of it—reaching out to schools and organizations to see if they need guest speakers or are interested in partnering. When I taught high school, I was trying to bring resources in and now I'm trying to extend resources out. When I guest speak, I bring students with me when possible, so that they can share their experiences and younger students can have exposure to college students. I love the model of university practicum classes where undergraduates go out into the community and teach, share, or work with younger students in an ongoing, systemic way where they can partner and build relationships.

The concept of community-responsive teaching grounds curriculum in the cultures and communities of schools. What does it look like when the community becomes an extension of the classroom and what would it be like for the schooling experience to be grounded in the community?

Classroom Application

A. What community organizations exist in your school neighborhood? Which might be useful to partner with for a project?
B. Invite a guest speaker from the community to speak about the work they do and how they got there.
C. Plan a fieldtrip.

Questions for Reflection or Discussion

1. What are the biggest challenges in your classroom, school, and community? Which are in your control? What can you do about those?

2. Community asset mapping. What resources and networks are in your community?

3. What units, projects, or assignments are students currently working on that would benefit from a guest speaker or community connection?

Bibliography

Chapman, G.D. (1995). *The five love languages: How to express heartfelt commitment to your mate*. Chicago: Northfield Publishing.

Cohen, D. (2016). *Capturing the Spark: Inspired Teaching, Thriving Schools*. Palo Alto, CA: Enactive Publishing.

Danielson, C. (2007). *Enhancing Professional Practice: A Framework for Teaching*. ASCD: Alexandria.

McCarthy, J. (2015, September 9). Student-Centered Learning: It Starts with the Teacher. *Edutopia*. Retrieved from https://www.edutopia. org/blog/student-centered-learning-starts-with-teacher-john-mccarthy

Pink, D. H. (2011). *Drive*. Edinburgh: Canongate Books.

Schnall, S., Harber, K. D., Stefanucci, J. K., & Proffitt, D. R. (2008). Social Support and the Perception of Geographical Slant. *Journal of Experimental Social Psychology*, 44(5), 1246–1255. https://doi. org/10.1016/j.jesp.2008.04.011

Yaron, L. (2014a, July 22). Five Tips for Real-World Teaching and Learning. *Education Week*. Retrieved from http://www.edweek.org/tm/ articles/2014/07/22/ctq_yaron_arts.html

Yaron, L. (2014b, May 14). Developing student support networks. *Education Week*. Retrieved from http://www.edweek.org/tm/ articles/2014/05/13/ctq-yaron-developing-student-support-networks.html

Yaron, L. (2013, April 23). Ten Ways to Pump Up the Volume on Student Leadership. *Education Week*. Retrieved from https://www.edweek. org/teaching-learning/opinion-ten-ways-to-pump-up-the-volume-on-student-leadership/2013/04

3

Foundation 3: Relevance

What does this have to do with me?

FIGURE 3.1

DOI: 10.4324/9781003318408-3

More than explicitly teaching anyone anything, intentional teaching creates the conditions for learning to occur. Rather than giving anyone knowledge, learning is a dynamic process that happens as a result of specific conditions. Students need to feel safe and supported in their environment. They need the resilience to adapt to various situations and the curiosity to learn from mistakes rather than avoid them. What they are learning needs to be enough of a stretch so that they're growing, and, at the same time, not too difficult that they shut down in the face of it. They need to believe that they can do it and that there is a reason for investing the effort they are putting in. They also need adequate schooling conditions and resources that reflect the value adults and society place on investing in their learning.

Schools and classrooms are structured by design—whether intentional or default—to produce a result. The more they are consciously constructed, the better chance there is for students to have the conditions they need to learn. Relevant schooling places students at the center of their learning experience. It meets students where they're at and bridges student culture with school culture in a safe classroom environment that honors student voice and individual identity. It recognizes the inner and outer challenges that students face and integrates cultural responsiveness, trauma-sensitivity, and emotional literacy into the curriculum, rather than as a separate add-on.

A. Culturally Responsive Teaching

Culturally responsive teaching situates students' identities and experiences at the center of their learning. It means a curriculum is grounded in the communities and lives of students. Rather than requiring students to adapt to school culture in order to access the curriculum, it meets students where they're at and bridges student culture with school culture through language, content, and instructional design. To teach my difficult ninth grade class, I could not muzzle their voices or hold the class too tightly—that would have restricted their room to grow and flattened engagement. I also couldn't hold it too loosely and let them run wild or they wouldn't have learned anything. It was a balance of listening to who they were, what styles of learning they required, what interested them, and what it took to create the conditions necessary for them to engage and learn. That was a vocal class, and I found that plays and poetry engaged them in performance and creative expression. Students remarked that they saw themselves reflected in August Wilson's characters and could relate to them. When they broke out in song to a beat and put his words into a rap, I allowed the flow of their voices and energy to guide the way. If I were to have taught a "traditional" class environment, I would have lost them and hated my job. It takes trust and a leap of faith to live in that balancing space as a teacher. And it can lead to the biggest rewards.

Culturally responsive teaching means examining the content that is taught, how it is taught, and how students interact with it. Whose voices are heard, whose are excluded? Are students reading from a diversity of authors and studying history of people from diverse backgrounds? Are they critically examining power structures and systems of inequities or simply being acted on by them? In my English class, we alternated between the lenses of race, class, and gender to view texts and characters. We read education theory and studied movements and individuals who worked toward equity and access. For our Spring Forum on Education project, students selected topics in schooling, created research questions, and presented on why elements of schooling are the way they are. Culturally responsive teaching means that students learn through a dynamic learning environment where they feel safe and supported to question, explore, create knowledge, build community, examine the systems and structures that exist, and have agency to work toward change. It isn't something that acts on students—it alchemizes to reflect students' lives and communities through engagement that makes it possible for them to learn.

A place to start is including a diversity of perspectives in the classroom. Though strategies for this are included here, it isn't meant to be a quick fix or displace or bypass the personal exploration that will lead to authentic approach and action. Tips include:

1. *Personal exploration.* Authentically engage with this topic on what it means for you as a teacher personally, coming from your own race, culture, and background. The book *Me and White Supremacy* by Layla F. Saad is a powerful book for White individuals on how to engage with race on a personal and actionable level. In it she writes, "It begins with being honest with yourself, getting educated, becoming more conscious about what is really going on (and how you are complicit in it), and getting uncomfortable as you question your core paradigms about race."

2. *Relevance.* Explore the purpose of why students are doing something from the standpoint of who they are. For example, I invite students to reflect on the question, "What does it mean to meditate as someone who identifies as _____?" It can be generalized to "What does it mean for you to be a student who identifies as _____?"

3. *Spotlight diverse voices.* Include a diversity of voices in the curriculum.

4. *Activities for multiple perspectives.* Create spaces where students can dialogue with each other, share perspectives, and build knowledge together.

5. *Diverse guest speakers.* Invite guest speakers from diverse perspectives and backgrounds.

6. *Share personal experiences.* As it applies, I share about being a first-generation Israeli American and what that meant for me in navigating the education system. Acknowledging race and culture and how it might have an impact (bias, privilege, access) makes it less invisible and normalizes conversations.

7. *Acknowledge collective events* or challenges as they arise. For example, acknowledging social justice protests and creating space for students to share what's coming up for them.

8. *Begin a topic with activating prior knowledge.* For example, asking them what _____ (freedom, mindfulness, race, etc.) is first before telling them a definition. A leading question can be, "What is your experience with_____?"

9. *Create space to share.* Invite discussion and conversation about diverse topics that honor student funds of knowledge in a safe space. Ask student opinions: "What do you think about_____?" "How is_____ going for you?"

10. *Inform students about diverse events* they might be interested in.

11. *Share resources.* As relevant, I might also share about a book I'm reading or something I came across. Or as it applies to the topic, I might say, "If you'd like to hear more about_____, I'd recommend the book/ person/podcast/website_____."

Inspired by George Ella Lyon's poem "Where I'm From," writing an "I Am From" poem is an accessible way of honoring student culture and identity. A student sample from my class is included here:

I am from pure blood of Mexican Raza pumping through my veins.
I am from a wall writing low rider hooping neighborhood.

I am from tacos, tamales, tortas, and quesadillas.

I am from getting into trouble, mom screaming out my whole name Federico Gonzalez Lopez Morales.

I am from parties on Saturday and recaluentas on Sunday.

I am from cumbias and salsa dancing music.

I am from a family of Mexican culture raised to show where I come from.

I am from a family raised to stand for what I believe in.

I am from a family running away down the hills searching for freedom, knowing America is freedom.

I am from a family struggling to be the best.

I am from a family giving love.

I am from a family that can't afford much.

I am from being raised to be proud of everything my parents do for me and my family.

I am from being raised in the ghetto apartment building where all my memories got started.

Sample Template:

I am from_____ (think back to the neighborhood you grew up in. What is it like? What do you see?)

I am from_____ (think back to the foods you ate growing up)

I am from_____ (describe your favorite things growing up)

I am from_____ (list a family tradition)

I am from_____ (what music did you hear? What is a song you remember?)

I am from_____ (what did you believe in?)

I am from_____ (describe your most memorable moments)

I am from_____ (describe your culture)

I am from_____ (list any sayings you heard growing up)

My book *Mindfulness for Young Adults: Tools to Thrive in School and Life* includes classroom inquiry questions around family, race, culture, gender, and sexuality. These questions can be a starting point for discussion and exploration. A selection of them are included here:

Family

- ◆ What role does family play in shaping who you are?
- ◆ How might early experiences influence your interactions with others?
- ◆ What might family dynamics have taught you about how to love, create healthy boundaries, or handle conflict?
- ◆ How might family have shaped ways of relating to intimacy and connection with self and others?

Race and Culture:

- ◆ What do you think race and/or culture is and how would you describe yours?
- ◆ What is the relationship you have with your racial and/or cultural heritage and the race/culture you are currently in? How does that dialogue evolve and differ across generations?
- ◆ What did your culture teach you about how to relate to hardships or emotions?
- ◆ What messages were communicated through culture about gender, race, or class?
- ◆ What is your favorite cultural tradition?

Gender and Sexuality:

- ◆ How do you relate to your gender?
- ◆ What stereotypes or traditional roles exist for different genders? Where might these stereotypes come from and how might they have contributed to your individual gender identity?

- ◆ What does it mean to have an empowered gender identity and what does it take to achieve it?
- ◆ How do you relate to your sexuality? What does it mean to have an empowered sexual identity and what does it take to achieve it?

Classroom Application

A. Ask students: What does it mean for you to be a student who identifies as _____?
B. Ask students to write an "I Am From" poem. Can be compiled into a class book.
C. Examine whose voices are included and not included in the curriculum.

Questions for Reflection or Discussion

1. What does it mean for you to be a teacher who (racially/ethnically/culturally) identifies as _____ teaching students who identify as _____?

2. Who are your students? What is their race, gender, background, community? How might it inform their experiences and perspectives?

3. What does a culturally relevant curriculum mean to you and what might it look like in your/the classroom?

B. Trauma-Sensitive Instruction

When I was starting out as a teacher, my administrator sat in on a class of mine where students were sharing their personal narratives. Often through tears, they spoke about challenges they faced in their lives, families, and communities. After class, the administrator remarked to me that my students needed counseling. Yes, they do. We all do. It is not an easy thing to be human, and that much more so for those who are struggling to get by, or coping with mental health challenges, or navigating the loss of family members and friends. Those who are in survival mode may not have the luxury of affording therapy, or may not come from a culture or family where therapy is acceptable yet, or may not know how to seek help.

Those students didn't have therapy, but they had me, and they had each other, and they had our time to come together and build resilience and skills that would help them thrive. This is not to say that teachers need to be therapists. I openly advocate for my students to seek therapy. And at the same time, we can learn to be responsive to student traumas and build supportive classroom communities that become protective factors to balance the risk factors of adverse experiences.

The CDC reports that adverse childhood experiences (including violence, abuse, neglect, home substance abuse, mental illness, and divorce) were reported to have been experienced by nearly two-thirds of adults surveyed across 25 states. One in six had experienced four or more types and people of color were found to have a disproportionately higher number of adversities and less access to professional care.

Given the challenges that students face, and particularly students of color, a component of culturally responsive teaching is emotional responsiveness to trauma. This includes the micro-traumas that occur each day, as well as the life-shifting macro traumas, like the death of a family member, violence, or abuse. Trauma can be acute in a one-time occurrence, chronic, or collectively faced by a group of people, such as the pandemic or racial injustice. Research in epigenetics shows that traumas can also be intergenerational, with both behavioral and genetic ways of operating in the world passed down to the next generation. Trauma can also be experienced secondarily or vicariously, where teachers and others may absorb the impact of student traumas. Incidentally, resilience can also be vicarious, where we can become more resilient in the face of the resilience of others. A trauma-sensitive curriculum doesn't mean that teachers become mental health professionals in the classroom—it means that the classroom becomes a safe community space for discussing challenges, building relationships and resilience, learning coping skills, and honoring the stories and struggles we carry with us.

Post-Traumatic Growth

More common than post-traumatic stress is post-traumatic growth, where we learn from our challenges and they help us grow stronger. I tell my students that while we sometimes cannot control what happens to us, we can choose how we respond to it, how we interact with it, how we make sense of it, and what we do next. Through our challenges, we can discover strengths we didn't know we had, and new opportunities may open for us. We may develop a deeper sense of appreciation for the lives we live, and greater meaning and purpose. Going through a struggle with someone can deepen relationships and remind us how important they are. It isn't about avoiding challenges—it's about how we can grow and learn from them. We cannot change the past, but we can choose how we view it, relate to it, and extract lessons from it.

The Buddha taught that there are two arrows to a traumatic moment: the first is the event, and the second is our reaction to it. It's the second arrow that is often more painful and the one where we have a possibility of choice. As humans, we have the capacity to let go or to hold on, for a very long time. With acceptance and kindness, we can learn to pull out the second arrow.

A student in my mindfulness course, Eric, was working on healing from his trauma. He shared with me a journal entry he wrote after a conversation we had after class. "My traumas are not me and I am not these traumas. My past doesn't define who I am. But my past has certainly shaped who I am today. My pain has cracked my heart open wide." He reflected that his pain allowed him to deepen relationships and made him more kind, compassionate, empathetic, understanding, honest, mature, and aware of joy. "I would not be the person I am today without my past." He acknowledged his pain, and also realized that he is so many more things than his trauma. It was something he experienced, but doesn't define who he is as a person. "There is so much more to me. I am much more than pain."

Psychologist James Pennebaker found that writing about stressful or traumatic events can help people process them and move forward. When we write, we organize our thoughts in a way that helps us understand and meaningfully come to terms with experiences. Finding meaning in trauma, as Eric did, helps to process events and move forward. Seeing the words from our challenges on paper helps to release the grip of the experience from the mind, as the brain's visual processing center sees the words on the page. We learn we don't have to hold our experiences so tightly. Harper, a student from my Stress Management for Healthy Living course, reflected about her journaling experience, "I felt a sense of calmness and relief from getting my thoughts out of my head and onto paper. There is something about getting my emotion or thought on paper that allows me to separate myself from it." Journaling helped her feel more in touch with who she is as a person. "I have learned how important it is to be gentle with myself and to not judge my thoughts or my emotions. I honestly didn't know that this kind of self-love was attainable for me."

When we express ourselves physically, emotionally, linguistically, or creatively, we release the thoughts and emotions from our experiences. Journaling, art, dance, and song are some forms of creative expression, though what works for someone might be different than what someone else needs. And what is needed in one situation might be different than what is needed in another. In the classroom, expression can be a vehicle for students to tune into their inner selves and identities.

Students may enter the classroom carrying shame and guarding their emotional selves. Shame is the internalizing and personalizing of *I am* bad, vs. the guilt of *I did something* bad or I made a mistake. We can learn to depersonalize and not identify student actions with labeling them as bad or good students, and we can also teach them to recognize when shame appears. As researcher Brené Brown advises, empathy is the antidote to shame. When we normalize experiences and emotions with activities like sharing personal stories and asking questions like "how many of you have ever felt...?" then we can start to lessen the grip of shame.

Also useful in building perspective here is teaching students to identify what psychologist Martin Seligman calls the "3 Ps" that stunt recovery from setbacks:

- *Personalization*, or the belief that we are at fault and there is something wrong with us. "How could I have let this happen? I'm so_____." Claiming his power in resisting this personalization rooted in shame, Eric noted, "There is nothing wrong with me ... I am worthy."
- *Pervasiveness*, or the belief that it will impact every area of our lives.
- *Permanence*, or the belief that it will impact us forever.

Years ago, I taught a high school senior who was a selective mute. She didn't speak in school following a traumatic experience as a child. My classes are discussion-based, and while I, of course, accommodated her based on her specialized learning plan, I also encouraged her to explore what it might be like to speak up. One day, when students were presenting on if they agreed or disagreed with Dostoyevsky's conclusion that freedom is the most advantageous advantage, she decided she would share the next day. She communicated to me that she would like to invite another teacher who had also been supportive of her. That day when it was her turn, she stood up, brought her notecard up to the front of class. And for the next thirty minutes opened and closed her mouth in silence, each time wanting to speak, but not yet able to do so. The class waited with her in silent support. She motioned to ask if she could turn to face the chalkboard, and then with tears streaming down her face, she did it. She shared. And the classroom erupted in applause after. It was such a courageous and vulnerable moment that we witnessed. One student gave her a card the next day telling her how inspiring it was. Years later, she emailed me to say that she talks now. This all was only possible in a supportive, safe classroom environment where student voices were honored and encouraged, and where expectations were high and supported. It is a balance of knowing how much to push and how much space to let them be in their comfort zone, and it takes knowing students and who they are and what motivates them to know the balance.

Secondary Trauma

As teachers, we are exposed to countless traumas—our own and also of those we teach and work with. In secondary trauma, or vicarious trauma, hearing firsthand about the traumas of others can take an emotional toll, particularly on educators, social workers, therapists, and others involved in the welfare of others. We may feel compassion fatigue from being there for others so much that it impacts our capacity to show up for ourselves.

Compassion is when we meet the suffering of others with kindness. Lately I've been trying to work on the nuance of *meeting* the challenges of others with kindness, rather than *holding* their challenges. I can meet it and show up, but not myself hold it. It's not mine to carry. Healthy boundaries are necessary, both emotionally and practically, to maintain a little distance between the situation and ourselves. This is not to say we do not care as deeply, or listen with as open a heart, or act with less kindness. This healthy distance helps us show up better for our students and ourselves—and makes the profession more sustainable for the long term. With all the challenges that teachers are exposed to, it is all that much more important to practice self-care and learn to cope, balance, and seek support when needed. While self-care is sometimes the first thing to go when caring for others, it is the most important thing that makes all other things possible. Put on your oxygen mask first. I know it's easy to say, and sometimes not as easy to do, but over time we can learn to minimize the impact of secondary trauma exposure to show up clearer for ourselves and our students. More on this in Chapter 4: Mental Health.

Classroom Application

A. Share about post-traumatic growth and the 3 P's. Ask students when they might have experienced them.
B. Practice journaling. Sample prompt: Write about a challenging experience that you overcame and that changed you into who you are today.
C. Create community through group opportunities for students to build relationships with each other.
D. Check in with students and ask how they are doing. If a student is going through something difficult, follow up to ask how they are holding up today.

Questions for Reflection or Discussion

1. What challenges and difficulties are experienced by your students? How might this impact their capacity to thrive?

2. What does trauma-sensitive teaching and learning mean to you and what does/might it look like in your school or classroom?

3. What do you do to release stress and trauma from the school day?

C. Application: Emotional Literacy

One factor that determines the capacity to thrive in education, career, and life is the ability to have awareness of our emotions and how to regulate them. This aspect of emotional intelligence underlies how we process and interact with the world. When we feel hurt, when we make mistakes, when we are in pain or stress, how do we meet it and hold it? How do we meet the pain of our students?

What to do with our feelings isn't often taught in schools, and yet students are informally tested on it more than any academic subject. They are often asked or expected to leave the outside world at the classroom door, but they need tools in how to do this in a healthy way that honors their experience, and at the same time holds them accountable to the professional space they're in. How to process life as it unfolds is not a simple skill. Yet the ability to manage emotions is a gatekeeper to success. Students who are not able to do so may shut down or tune out to what's happening in the classroom. On the opposite end, others may amp up in distraction and restlessness. Students may try to numb their feelings with substance use or develop depression or anxiety not knowing how to cope with the very real challenges they face and how they relate to their feelings.

Culturally responsive teaching includes emotionally responsive teaching, not as an add-on to the already full plate of teachers, but an integration and vehicle to help students access the academic content. "I realize that my academic success can be very reflective of what's going on internally and that in order for me to succeed to the best of my ability, I found that I need to really take time to care for my mental health," reflected Leilani, as she spoke about our mindfulness course in a Diversity, Equity, Inclusion Week student panel.

Emotionally responsive teaching includes a sensitivity to understanding the lives and challenges that students face, both in and out of the classroom. It means teaching awareness tools to deal with the complex emotions of what it means to be human and to be them. It means placing the cultures and the students we teach at the center of the curriculum, with the classroom as a bridge between a student's culture and the culture of schooling. How do we hold, process, and respond to our emotions and the emotions of those around us?

As an educator, I came to realize that if I was to be able to teach academic literacy skills, then my teaching would need to be responsive to the cultures, challenges, traumas, and emotions that my students faced. If my classroom was to truly create conditions for my students to thrive, then I needed to create a community space where they were able to share their challenges and build emotional literacy skills alongside the academic content. The mental health challenges students and teachers faced through the pandemic magnified the importance of intentionally supporting socioemotional learning. Lena, a student in my mindfulness course, noticed that building emotional literacy tools helped her be more responsive. "I feel that I am more open and also more mindful of my emotions and how they play an important role in my health." She noticed she felt calmer and less reactive toward her emotions. "I don't let them overpower me. Instead, I listen to them and determine what is the best response to it."

Situating emotional literacy alongside academic studies explicitly teaches tools to navigate life challenges. It is not something that somehow happens. It is built through intention matched with purposeful action. This is, of course, not to say that students do not already possess a wealth of resources in coping with emotions, but that through targeted practices it is possible to grow emotional literacy in the same way we might grow academic literacy skills. At the broader school level, this can include structuring supports into the school day—not as an additional thing to add to the already full plate of teachers, but as a shift in the way we think about the plate itself. At a schoolwide level, this can take the form of well-being courses, guest speakers, curriculum projects, awareness days, student clubs, after-school and lunchtime sessions, or including quality professional development in well-being supports, mental health, and emotional literacy. Teacher education programs can include pedagogy on emotionally responsive, trauma-sensitive curriculum as a component of culturally responsive teaching. To teach cultural responsiveness is to include the challenges that students face on an emotional and mental health level, both collectively and personally.

This is not separate from teaching academic content, but a vehicle for it. In a Fall 2019 survey of my Introduction to Mindfulness courses at the USC, 41% of students said that the course much or very much impacted their studying or grades—whether breaths to calm their nerves before an exam, mindful study breaks, or coping with difficult emotions that arose with learning academic content. "As I was getting frustrated while studying, I had this other option, which many times while studying you feel that there is no other option," Devin, a sophomore business major, reflected. He found that meditation gave him a perspective and assurance that he would be okay and learn the material in time. "Many times, I would just quit, but this time even a little step away from the desk can reshape your entire perspective on the situation."

A junior in my mindfulness class, Philip, was a serial procrastinator. Every assignment was turned in late. He admitted that this was how he operated across classes through his schooling. I invited him to explore the underlying cause of his procrastination and suggested he bring mindful awareness to it. He came to realize his relationship between stress and procrastination. He observed that procrastination was a coping response to his stress. "For me, stress is one of the causes of procrastination," he reflected. "When the tasks in front of me seem insurmountable, procrastinating adversely allows me to not think about the stressful things I need to get done." Through learning to identify his emotions and work with them more skillfully, he was able to use alternative, healthier coping mechanisms. "If I can just take ten minutes to meditate and sit with my feelings of stress and anxiety and whatever else, then the obstacles in front of me do become more surmountable, and I can break things down into bite size pieces and formulate strategies to overcome them, rather than simply procrastinate to suppress the not great feelings they create." For all the teachers who have had to remind Philip to turn in late assignments through his schooling, what a breakthrough for him to realize that he can have a healthier response to stress through building emotional literacy tools.

As schools and districts step into this new era in education, it is not just a luxury, but a core component of schooling to think about how we intentionally include well-being, mental health, and emotional supports for students and teachers. What does it take for our students to thrive in school and life? What tools and conditions do teachers need so that their students can access the academic content in a way that is sustainable and meaningful? On taking a mindfulness course in her school schedule, Ellie, a senior business major, reflected, "Having this class and going through academics at the same time, it was kind of like a constant reminder to check-in with myself and see what I needed, and it made space for self-care and reflection." She was able to intentionally check in with herself through the semester to ensure she was doing things that helped her de-stress, like spending time with friends, meditating, and exercising. In doing this, she reflected, "I was able to actually be more productive in my classes and just show up better in my relationships and my classes and be less stressed overall. Basically, it just helped me create this habit of balance and showed me the power of having balance."

RAIN Technique for Working with Emotions

Mindfulness techniques can help build resilience in students as they learn how to navigate challenges and breathe through them to emerge stronger on the other side. Teaching students to label what they're feeling, and trust that they have the capacity to breathe through it, emboldens them with the freedom to know that they can face whatever comes their way. Research shows that this task of naming an emotion, or affect labeling, is an effective technique for decreasing reactivity and the charge around difficult emotions. "By labeling them (emotions), acknowledging them, and allowing them to pass, they have become easier to deal with. I know these thoughts don't make me," reflected Shandra, a public relations major. Before taking our mindfulness class, she didn't think much about her mental health, and used to brush off or suppress unpleasant feelings. "I now feel comfortable speaking about the things that bother me with my mom and close friends and have even set up sessions to speak to professionals about my mental health."

Rather than pushing emotions away, being overwhelmed by them, or acting out of habit, default, or reactivity, we can learn to choose a conscious response. In the midst of all the busyness and emotions students and teachers experience in a day, we can take a moment to pause, notice, and breathe. This can help calm the nervous system and bring it into a state of receptivity rather than defensiveness or reactivity. Label the emotion, whether anger or love, joy or pain, fear or trust. Next, allow the emotion without trying to resist, push, away, or make it into anything else. Notice where the emotion might be sitting in the body, whether in the abdomen, chest, throat, or head. Notice the qualities that the emotion embodies. Is it heavy or light? Hot or cold? Sharp or dull? Moving fast or slow? What is the felt sensation of the emotion? Try to release identification to it by relating to it as *the* emotion, rather than *my* emotion (*the* impatience rather than *my* impatience). This creates space to not take the emotion personally, knowing that emotions come and go and pass through us all the time. We are not our emotions; they don't define who we are. They are temporary states that are part of the human experience. Nurture yourself in the moment and hold what arises with kindness. This technique is called RAIN:

RAIN Technique

Recognize and label the emotion.
Allow and accept it instead of pushing it away.
Investigate how it feels in the body.
Nurture to hold what arises with kindness and
   non-identification (*the* emotion, rather than *my* emotion).

We can learn to process and metabolize emotions through working with them in this way. We don't need to forcefully try to let go of an emotion, but through this work can get a little space around and from them so that they don't need to hold on so tightly. Incorporating mindful awareness practices into the classroom can help students learn to regulate their emotions so that when difficult ones like shame, anger, or anxiety arise, they can pause, notice the emotion, and have a skillful, rather than reactive, response. It can also help with cultivating well-being practices like gratitude, equanimity, and savoring joy. This helps students gain a sense of power and control necessary for self-actualization and is a pathway to greater emotional stability, resilience, and mental health. More mindfulness techniques are included in Chapter 4: Mental Health. A student in my mindfulness class reflected, "I feel like I am more stable with my emotions and aware of what I am feeling on the day-to-day." Another found that mindfulness "provided me with the ability to receive and find awareness, regardless of what situations and events may occur in daily life."

Emotional Conditions for Learning

Affective filter refers to the emotional or psychological screens or filters that may obscure learning. Creative and critical thinking are optimized when the stress response is lowered and students' minds and bodies are at ease. When students feel safe and feel like they can thrive in an environment, they are more likely to learn. They will not be able to learn to their fullest capacity when they are hungry, stressed, tired, anxious, afraid, or preoccupied with other things. The stress response narrows their physiological and mental functioning. An element of the polyvagal theory developed by Stephen Porges, neuroception describes the unconscious mental process of scanning for threats to determine if we are safe. The vagus nerve that runs from the base of the brain to the base of the spine is connected to our internal organs and nervous system. One way to settle the nervous system and build vagal nerve tone is through taking slow, deep breaths. Other strategies include exercise, meditation, humming, or through physical touch, including giving oneself a hand massage or hug. Settling the nervous system allows the mind to release preoccupation with safety and expend energy on learning instead of self-preservation.

With the broaden-and-build theory, psychologist Barbara Fredrickson's research shows that when we lower stress and cultivate more positivity to relax our minds, we can see more broadly and envision more creative options. In schools that encourage the 4 C's of critical thinking, collaboration, creativity, and communication, teaching students to cope with stress is a necessary component of broadening their scope and depth of possibilities. Though teachers are tasked with teaching subject areas, in order to do so, it often means they may need to look at what gets in the way of learning. This includes explicitly identifying and addressing affective filters so that students can fully learn and thrive. It may be through taking a few breaths to start or end class, teaching students to notice and label emotions, and creating a welcoming classroom container where students feel safe to participate and take risks. This is not to apply a quick fix or bypass the very real safety concerns that students have, or to make feeling psychologically safe seem easy, but to say that there are practical things we can do to intentionally create an environment more conducive to learning through looking at what might get in the way.

Classroom Application

A. Take a few breaths together to start and end class.
B. Teach students how to notice and label emotions.
C. Teach the RAIN technique for working with emotions.

Questions for Reflection and Discussion

1. What emotions come up for you and your students in the classroom? How do you typically cope with them?

2. What does emotional reactivity look like in the classroom?

3. What does emotionally responsive teaching and learning mean to you and what does/might it look like in your school or classroom?

Bibliography

Baicker, K. (2020, March 12). The impact of secondary trauma on educators. ASCD. Retrieved from https://www.ascd.org/el/articles/the-impact-of-secondary-trauma-on-educators

Barrett, L. F. (2017). *How emotions are made: The secret life of the brain.* New York: Houghton Mifflin Harcourt.

CDC. (2019). *Adverse childhood experiences.* Retrieved from www.cdc.gov/violence/prevention/childabuseandneglect/acestudy/index.html

Felitti, V.J. (2002). The relation between adverse childhood experiences and adult health: Turning gold into lead. *Permanente Journal, 6*(1), 44–47. https://www.ncbi.nlm.nih.gov/pmc/articles/PMC6220625/

Fredrickson, B. (2009). *Positivity: Top-notch research reveals the upward spiral that will change your life.* New York: Harmony.

Germer, C.K. (2009). *The mindful path to self-compassion: Freeing yourself from destructive thoughts and emotions.* New York: Guilford Press.

Jennings, P.A. (2018). *The trauma-sensitive classroom: Building resilience with compassionate teaching.* New York: W.W. Norton & Company.

Ladson-Billings, G. (1995). But That's Just Good Teaching! The Case for Culturally Relevant Pedagogy. *Theory into Practice, 34*(3), 159–165. http://www.jstor.org/stable/1476635

Levine, P. (2010). *In an unspoken voice: How the body releases trauma and restores goodness.* Berkeley: North Atlantic Books.

Porges, S. (2004). Neuroception: A subconscious system for detecting threats and safety. *Zero to Three, 24*(5), 19–24.

Post Traumatic Growth Research Group Site. Retrieved from https://ptgi.uncc.edu

Tedeschi, R. G., & Calhoun, L. G. (1996). The Posttraumatic Growth Inventory: measuring the positive legacy of trauma. *Journal of Traumatic Stress, 9*(3), 455–471. https://doi.org/10.1007/BF02103658

Terrasi, S., & de Galarce, P.C. (2017). Trauma and learning in America's classrooms. *Phi Delta Kappan, 98*(6), 35–41. https://doi.org/10.1177/0031721717696476

Treleaven, D., & Willoughby, B. (2018). *Trauma-sensitive mindfulness: Practices for safe and transformative healing.* New York: W.W. Norton & Company.

Van der Kolk, B. (2014). *The body keeps the score: Brain, mind, and body in the healing of trauma.* New York: Viking Press.

4

Foundation 4: Mental Health

Mental health and resilience are explored in the next two chapters in an integrated approach to whole body well-being. This is not meant to be an exhaustive account, but rather an exploration of key factors that influence these components and practical approaches that can be applied in the classroom and life.

How can I flourish and stay centered?

FIGURE 4.1

DOI: 10.4324/9781003318408-4

A. Mindfulness in Physical, Mental, and Social Well-Being

Despite best intentions to create healthy school spaces, they are often driven by rushed bells, with large volumes of material to cover and stressful, high-stakes assessments. They are likely not equipped to address student crises, they serve varying degrees of unhealthy food, involve large amounts of sitting, and ask for more hours than exist in a day in order to effectively do one's job. This is true for students and those who teach them.

Yet this doesn't have to be the case. Schools can be nourishing, healthy environments for those in them. Seriously. Structuring schools so that well-being supports exist alongside academics isn't an extra component on top of already full teacher plates. It's the vehicle to support student learning and lives. When students are physically, mentally, and emotionally nourished, they can fully thrive. When teachers have the space and time for self-care practices within healthy, sustainable work conditions, they can flourish and don't have to choose between their health and their jobs.

Mindfulness involves conscious, present awareness in a way that is kind, curious, and accepting of what is happening. Acceptance here doesn't mean passivity. It's a willingness to be with our experiences in what's happening when it's happening. It is a courageous practice to be with our human experience and all the thoughts, emotions, and sensations that arise. It offers a freedom and responsiveness to choose how we show up for ourselves, others, and the world around us. It can be practiced formally in meditation or informally in bringing awareness into daily life, relationships, communication, decision making, and how we operate in the world. Imagine what schools might be like if they led with present, kind, open, curious awareness.

The preamble to constitution of the World Health Organization declares health to be a "state of complete physical, mental, and social well-being and not merely the absence of disease or infirmity." Recognizing the interconnected components of mind-body health, we can be as intentional with mental and social well-being as we would with physical health and discuss them as interrelated parts of a whole body system. Bringing mindful awareness to these elements in the classroom and life can help us all flourish.

Physical Health

A high school senior, Jacob, was often distracted in my English class and couldn't sit still or focus. In my Healthy Lifestyles course, he got tired easily and was unable to complete a lap around the track. One day, he told me he went to the doctor because he was having trouble sleeping. His doctor prescribed him sleeping pills. I asked him about his diet, and he mentioned he didn't drink water because he didn't like the taste of it. He only drank Coke. All day. He was so hyped up on sugar that he couldn't concentrate in class, and he couldn't sleep at night. We talked about gradually adding in a glass of water each day, with a little lemon for taste. He ultimately ended up getting off soda—and the sleeping pills. He had so much more energy to run and was able to focus and thrive in class. This was possible because we identified what it was that was causing his distraction. If I had only focused on the academics, I would have missed it. Imagine if he continued on this path of soda and sleeping pills rather than fixing the root of the issue. To teach students means to teach the whole child, not just part of them. What is it that they need in order to thrive? What is getting in their way? How can they build empowerment tools to take charge of their bodies, minds, and learning?

Basic principles of exercise, nutrition, and sleep can play an important role in balancing body and mind. It isn't a quick fix or to discount the countless other factors that impede learning, or to place yet another role on teachers, but to say that these principles of healthy living can make a difference—both in our lives and the personal and academic lives of our students.

Exercise

Sitting all day in classroom chairs is counter to what young bodies (or any bodies) need. Exercise has been shown to have a tremendous impact on whole body and mind function. It can help boost mood, discharge stress, aid in sleep, and increase overall health and well-being. Exercising with others and on team sports can build relationships, community, and a sense of belonging. Some tips for schools:

♦ Ask students to identify physical movement exercises they enjoy.

♦ Practice mindful walking to help students notice their surroundings. Walking without a phone in hand, they can learn to turn into their senses of what they see and hear, noticing how it feels to walk and move in their bodies.

♦ Set group goals for exercise. Make them SMART (specific, measurable, attainable, realistic, and in a timeframe).

♦ Check in and celebrate success.

♦ Create a schoolwide health challenge.

Nutrition

My trash can was constantly filled with empty Hot Cheetos bags by end of the school day. What students eat is the fuel in their tanks. Nutrients help them be mentally alert and able to learn. Contrary to what some may think, it is possible to eat healthy foods that are cheap and easy to prepare. It also takes some effort to learn how to do it. A few things I've found to be helpful in the classroom:

♦ Make a recipe book. Each student submits a healthy, easy, recipe for a class book. They can also include the story behind the recipe or interview a family member to learn about a recipe.

♦ Partner with a community organization to come in for recipe demos of healthy, easy recipes using affordable ingredients.

♦ Keep a food log to track food intake. It can include how the body and energy felt after eating.

♦ Practice mindful eating. Take the time to notice each bite, the sensations it brings, and focus on the singular experience of eating.

Sleep

As a teen and college student, I normalized being tired. Like many other young adults going to bed late and waking up early, I wasn't getting all the sleep my body needed in its developmental stage. It wasn't until I got older that I discovered it was totally possible to go through the day well-rested. And it felt so great. Sleep is helpful for cognitive function, decision-making, restoring the body and immune system, and overall well-being. Sleep hygiene tips include:

- ◆ Set regular sleep and wake times.
- ◆ Avoid large meals, alcohol, bright lights, and screen time before bed.
- ◆ Wind down with a calming nighttime routine, like meditation, reading, journaling, or taking a warm shower. This helps create a separation from the day and signals to the body that it's time to rest.

Consent

In sharing resilience stories in class, a high school senior shared that she was sexually assaulted at a party she went to. That moment jolted me to think about what I wasn't doing and could be doing in the classroom to speak about consent and assault. A different student from that same class told me years later that she was assaulted at a party her freshman year of college. We worked so hard to get her to college but couldn't protect her so that she was safe there. And it is so common. Every year I've taught at university, someone will share a story of sexual assault when we share resilience stories. For all that we do to prepare students academically, what does it all mean if they are unsafe? Of undergraduates, the Rape, Abuse & Incest National Network (RAINN) estimates that 26.4% of females and 6.8% of males experience rape or sexual assault through physical force, violence, or incapacitation. This is not an individual issue to be solved by telling students to stay together with friends at a party or watch their drink so someone doesn't put something in it. The magnitude shows us this is a systemic issue, and systemic issues need to be solved structurally and culturally alongside individual and collective action.

We start the dialogue with the question, "What does consent mean to you?" and open a space to share about the topic. Students reflect that consent means that all parties consciously agree to a single encounter. They note the difference between asking, "Is this OK?" and "This is OK, right?" They share that just because something happens once, it doesn't mean that it gives free rein to happen again. We talk about the difference between a lowercase sort of "yes" and "**YES**" in radical consent, noticing how different forms of yes or no feel in the body. I then pose the question "what can we do to create a culture of consent on campus?" to dialogue about what this means, who is responsible, and what we can all do.

Substance Use

In class we also discuss the power of making conscious decisions around what we choose to put in our bodies. Not in a preachy way, but in building self-awareness. A student in my mindfulness class, Vivian, reflected about her decision to quit e-cigarettes, "With the scary evidence of the consequences of vaping staring me right in the face, I realized that I myself needed to stop harming my body immediately. Breaking any kind of addiction is difficult, but I discovered that my routine/practice of mindfulness could be used to my advantage to help me." Mindfulness helped her change her thoughts toward nicotine so she could have more freedom to make conscious decisions. "The choice of a healthy body and expelling an addiction to something resonated stronger in my heart and my mind rather than a life influenced by shame and fear through addiction. ... Two years later, I feel lighter physically and emotionally through lifting the burden of addiction off my shoulders." Through mindful self-awareness we can learn to break unconscious habits and align decisions with values. This is the freedom to live our lives as we choose, aware and awake, and not have them dictated by unconscious habit.

Mental Health

We can build mental health in the same way we can build physical health and can normalize it through creating space in curriculum and discussion. Students felt so much agency after our Mental

Health Video and Research Project that they created a school Mental Health Club and hosted schoolwide activities like lunchtime yoga classes and events, including a schoolwide assembly. As part of the Mikva Challenge Action Civics Showcase, they shared their voices and ideas with students from across the city dialoguing about issues of importance. They took action around a topic that was meaningful to them and learned to normalize the dialogue and practices for building mental health. I start the discussion by asking, "What are things you do to care for your mental health?" Responses include exercising, spending time with friends, being in nature, and journaling (all things that research has shown to be helpful).

The National Alliance for Mental Illness (NAMI) reports that 75% of mental health conditions begin before the age of 24. High school and college are foundational times for students as they learn to build mental health tools. Year after year, my students entered the classroom with traumas and challenges that impacted their ability to be fully present and open to the academic curriculum. It soon became clear that it was necessary to address socioemotional needs alongside building academic skills if they were to fully access the curriculum and thrive to their highest potential. I needed to attend to what was happening in their hearts alongside teaching them to build skills with their minds. But I struggled with how to do it in a tangible, sustainable, systemic, and scalable way with the means available. Mindfulness offers a framework for not just what we do, but also how we do it. It provides a common language and process for how we can skillfully work with challenges and open fully to our experiences.

Mindfulness

Through mindfulness we can learn to relate to our present-moment experiences with kindness, openness, curiosity, compassion, and acceptance. What does it mean to be present for what is happening when it's happening—in the classroom, in the world, and in ourselves? When difficulties arise, it can be easy to ignore or push away big feelings that come with them. There is a power and freedom in learning how to respond, rather than react, to events. In challenging times, it's not what happens that makes the most difference in our outcomes—it's how we deal with what happens, what we believe about it, and what we do with it. We can practice skills for what to do in times of difficulty to transform challenging experiences into opportunities for growth. Mindful awareness practices can help us notice our emotions, thoughts, and bodies in the midst of our experiences. How do we relate to the moments of our lives, whether times of joy or discomfort, and how do we hold our experiences with openness and curiosity instead of distraction and judgment? How do we show up to be present for ourselves and in interactions with others?

Simply taking a moment to pause, whether at the start or end of class, or in a big moment, can go a long way in finding more ease and grounding. The mindfulness technique STOP can help us to pause, notice, and focus attention. *Stop* for a moment amid whatever is happening. *Take a breath*; take a few breaths. Slow, deep breaths send a signal of calm to the nervous system. Breath is a resource we can turn to at any time to help us make it through, one moment at a time. *Observe* what is happening inside of you. What sensations in the body, emotions, or thoughts might be present? Take a moment to set an intention or think of how you want to *proceed* from that point forward.

STOP Technique

Stop and pause.
Take a breath; take a few breaths.
Observe what might be happening inside you—any sensations in the body, emotions, or thoughts.
Proceed and think of how you want to move forward from that point onwards.

It can be difficult to pause and notice what's arising in challenging times. As technologically plugged in as this generation of students is, it's very easy to turn to a phone, video game, music, or other mode of distraction or numbing. Instead, we can teach them to honor their experience, hold it with kindness and attention, and make a conscious decision as to how they want to go forward.

Students who have experienced trauma may have a particularly difficult time tuning into their experience and body. It takes safety and trust to sit with eyes closed and notice what's arising. It may be helpful to offer alternatives, like keeping their eyes open and fixed on one spot, rather than eyes closed. Or feeling their feet grounded on the floor and staying with the grounding sensation. Perhaps alternating between the emotion arising and the sensations of the feet or another anchoring home base. Another technique is to choose a safe place or kind person to visualize sitting next to them. Mindfulness can offer freedom and space in the present moment, but it can also be triggering as emotions arise. Not every practice is going to work for each person and it's important to work with our bodies and meet ourselves where we're at. It is a good idea to go gently and slowly so as to avoid flooding or overwhelming the body, mind, and heart with more than it can handle at the time.

Tips for building a meditation practice: Pick a place and time of the day to practice. Many people prefer practicing in the morning to set the tone for the day, or before bed to unwind from the day. Set a realistic goal for an allotted amount of time (perhaps five to ten minutes if just starting out). Even a little bit can make a difference. As for posture, if sitting in a chair, sit comfortably so that your thighs are parallel to the floor, adding a pillow or blanket under your feet or on the seat as necessary. If sitting on the floor, sit cross-legged with a cushion underneath you if your knees are higher than your hips. Sit with the crown on the head lifted with a quality that is bold and alert, yet relaxed. In addition to the STOP technique, a body scan meditation or focusing on the breath are two other useful practices to begin with.

Working with thoughts in meditation: Just like learning any skill, through diligent practice over time, we can get better at being more present and working with our thoughts and emotions in skillful ways that create a little more space and freedom. The mind will naturally wander, and it can be surprising to realize how many thoughts are present, how quickly they come, and how easy it is to get hooked into the stories of them. Through mindfulness, we can nonjudgmentally notice thoughts without getting attached to them, and gently bring our attention back to the present moment. It's not that thinking is bad—thoughts helped us get to where we are by reflecting on the past and planning for the future. On an evolutionary level, thinking and scanning for threats and opportunities helped our ancestors survive. And yet, we can explore what type of thoughts are useful and when it is useful to follow them. We can make a conscious choice to not get lost in the storyline of our thoughts in meditation and redirect attention toward a home base. Using the breath, body, or sound as an anchor, we can return to that home base as a way of grounding our attention in the present moment. This allows us to open to our experience exactly as it is, without trying to resist or make it into anything else. When thoughts arise, we can ask, "Is this useful?" "Is this true?" And we can choose to return back to the breath, body, and moment as an anchor rather than be hooked in our unconscious storyline and get lost in thought.

Mindfulness is not a silver bullet, or quick fix for mental health issues, or replacement for therapy. It is a tool that can help us build awareness, equanimity, and space to choose a conscious response to what is happening.

Social Health

As humans, we are hardwired for connection. This is something we can actively grow and construct in our lives. In a longitudinal study that began in the 1930s of 238 Harvard men, psychologist George Vaillant remarked in 2009, "70 years of evidence that our relationships with other people matter, and matter more than anything else in the world." He summarized the outcome of the study with the words, "Happiness is love. Full stop." Relationships take many forms, including friends, family, co-workers, partners, acquaintances, colleagues, and students. How we acknowledge and tend to our relationships and interactions with others can have a significant impact on our lives and theirs, as a multitude of studies reveal that social connections and community can have a positive impact on health and well-being. Setting the time and intention to connect can be as simple as saying hello, reaching out and asking how someone is, deeply and actively listening to what people say, seeking ways to help, expressing gratitude for something someone said or did, or celebrating the successes of friends.

In times of stress, we may reach out to others, and when they reach out to us, seek to comfort them. Psychologist Shelley Taylor calls this the "tend and befriend" response to stress. She writes, "one of the most striking aspects of the human stress response is the tendency to affiliate—that is, to come together in groups to provide and receive joint protection in threatening times." Part of the stress response includes the release of bonding hormones that drive us toward social support and connection during stressful times. Mindfulness can help us deepen relationships and communication by being fully present with others in speaking and listening. We can learn to bring our whole selves to our interactions and show up with openness and authenticity as we relate to ourselves and one another.

In the classroom, we can construct opportunities for community building through cooperative groups so students can dialogue and get to know each other. Strategic grouping can enhance learning, not just through hearing the ideas of others and working together, but through social support and connection that can bring students out of the stress response and into their present experiences. In a structured relational mindfulness pair activity, I have students ask each other the repeated question, "What made you into who you are today?" After hearing the answer, the questioner responds, "Thank you," in simple appreciation and acknowledgement. The questioner then repeats, "What made you into who you are today?" After five minutes of this process, they switch who is answering and asking the question. The repeated question allows students to go deeper in exploration of the answer. The "thank you" allows students to simply listen without trying to think of what to say in response. It is a safe receiving and holding of the response. After the activity, a student commented that they can spend six months in classes with others and not really know them, but this activity allowed them to see each other on a deeper level.

With our colleagues, we become part of a community of teachers who are all in this together. Positive relationships with peers and adults can be a protective factor for students (and all of us). The classroom becomes a safe container to dialogue about issues, build relationships, and explore purpose and identity. We can learn to see and listen to one another and create spaces where students feel seen and heard, while they learn tools to navigate challenges together.

Physical, mental, and social well-being are interconnected, and all contribute to our overall health. Francis, an English major, wrote in a mindfulness course reflection, "I can sincerely say I feel the strongest I've ever felt, physically, mentally and emotionally." She now takes the time to go to the gym and do physical activity at least five days a week. "I meditate, and I try to approach conflicts with a mindful viewpoint and attitude. This class has changed the way I function within all my relationships for the better, including the relationship I have with myself."

Classroom Application

A. Ask students what they do to care for their physical, mental, and social health.
B. Set goals for enhancing physical, mental, and social health.
C. Ask students to discuss what consent means to them.

Questions for Reflection or Discussion

1. What are things you do to care for your physical health? Mental health? Social health?

2. How healthy do you think your students are across the areas of physical, mental, and social well-being?

3. What's something you can do to increase healthy living in your curriculum, classroom, or school?

B. Stress Resilience

Schools can be stressful places. While what is especially needed is systems-wide learning and working conditions that collectively reduce external stress, recognizing that we can't wait that long, this section focuses on how to cope on an individual level. Typically, the nervous system vacillates between the sympathetic (on) and parasympathetic (rest) nervous system. In stressful times, the system may be continuously activated without rest and stuck on "on," or it may stay stuck in the "off" mode. In the classroom, this can show up as either hypervigilance/overactivity or the student who shuts down.

Learning tools to cope with stressors and build stress resilience can lead to increased performance in the classroom and more ease in life. It can start with a discussion of the things that cause stress and the options we have when responding to stressors. My Stress Management for Healthy Living course at USC started with a "Stress Share," where a student shares about a stress or challenge they are facing or have faced. They include how they are coping and lessons learned. This creates a climate where we normalize discussions around stress and share coping strategies to build collective resilience.

What Is Stress?

Stress manifests as a response to external or internal stimuli that activates the sympathetic nervous system. Realizing that it's a response within rather than a tangible object outside of ourselves, we can learn to find skill and space in how we respond to stress. In her book *The Upside of Stress*, health psychologist Kelly McGonigal defines stress as "what arises when something we care about is at stake." She refers to the physiological response of stress as our body's way of mobilizing resources to help us rise to the challenge. She writes, "Rather than determining once and for all 'is stress bad?' or 'is stress good?', I am now most interested in understanding how the stance we take toward stress matters. A better question for each of us to ask ourselves, as individuals trying to cope with stress, might be: *Do I believe I have the capacity to transform stress into something good?"*

When we are faced with challenges, and the difficult emotions that accompany them, we have options. We can plow through, shut down, face it, or pause and sit with what's arising. In challenging times, it's not what happens that makes the most difference in our outcomes, it's how we deal with what happens, what we believe about it, and what we do with it. Stress isn't just something that passively happens to us, it is something that alchemizes with our awareness and care and can transform into strength, wisdom, patience, and compassion.

This is not to discount the very stressful conditions of schools or to apply a quick fix. It isn't to say that the solution to the stressful state of schools is for teachers and students to learn to get better at stress. It is essential to create conditions that reduce stress on a schoolwide and systems level, and at the same time there are things we can do meanwhile to bring a little more ease. Viewing the stress response in this way is not to say that harmful stressful situations should be endured. Adverse situations should be assessed with wise discernment to choose to take action to change or leave a situation that is causing harm. Counselors, trusted friends, or advisors can aid in this process. What this means is that we can learn to be aware and mindful of how to listen to and navigate the feelings that arise around stress and make a conscious choice in how we show up to meet the moment.

Stress often appears as constriction and tension that grips in the body, perhaps in the abdomen, chest, or throat. In a time of stress, we can locate the feeling in the body, and perhaps envision the space around it. We can ask, "Where am I constricted in this situation? Where can I find a little freedom?" The stress is then forced to share space in the body with awareness, lessening its power as we bring the unconscious to light and name it. Emotional granularity is the concept of accurately naming the aspect of an umbrella emotion such as stress. We can try to accurately discern what it is we're really experiencing—rushed with too much to do in too little time, fear of the future or failure, pressure to perform well, too many people who all want something different from us at the same time, or whatever it may be. Getting clear on the emotion underlying stress helps us to accurately work with it.

In a moment of stress, we can also ask, "What am I not seeing clearly?" or "What do I know for sure?" or "What is it that I care about in this situation?" When stress narrows our focus, we may miss important information that can help us get perspective on the stimulus or desired outcome. When we zoom out, we may realize that we have more time than we thought, that there is another way of doing it, or we can reframe it to our advantage. Studies have found that when people interpreted the stress response as a resource that aids performance they actually did perform better. During stressful times, the body mobilizes all its energy to help us rise to the challenge—focus narrows, the heart beats faster, and blood rushes to extremities to help us perform. We can breathe in these moments and learn to recognize the physiological stress response as our body's mechanism of helping us take action. A study on reappraising performance anxiety showed that when participants reframed "I'm so nervous" into "I'm so excited," they performed better. When I told my students about this technique before a presentation, they remarked that it did actually help them feel more relaxed. In times of nerves, we can reframe it, tell ourselves "I'm so excited," and remind ourselves that we have what it takes to do our best.

Though we can't eliminate stress from life, what we can do is learn to get better at working with it through recognizing it as a messenger of information. We can start to free its grip, loosen the slack, and discover the freedom to choose a response.

Growth Mindset

In working with stress, we can cultivate a growth mindset approach to challenges. Psychologist Carol Dweck's research on fixed versus growth mindsets found that we can create the mindset and conditions to thrive when we focus on what we can learn and how we can grow our skills to become better. On the other hand, when we approach tasks or challenges in a fixed way of thinking that we are either bad or good at something, then we limit our growth. Applied to the stress response, we can learn to get better at stress and grow our capacity to effectively respond to challenging situations or emotions.

When we notice the stress response arising, we can learn to take a breath, pause, and then make a decision of how to best navigate the circumstance. We can learn tools to discharge stress and train ourselves to choose responsiveness over reactivity. Though some people may have a baseline range of stress that might make them more prone to anxiety, we can actually shift our stress response effectiveness and modulate the intensity and duration of the charged feelings through practicing how to work with stress. We can achieve growth in how we cope with stressors and challenges though placing our attention and focus on becoming better at them. Each experience is another opportunity to train our minds to become more skilled at navigating challenges. We get better at stress through targeted practice with effort and attention.

Physiological Response

Our ancestors required instinctual physical responses to the threats that jeopardized their survival. Over time, humans genetically developed a complex interaction of nerves, muscles, hormones, organs, and other bodily systems to deal with these stressors, and then return the body back to balance. The stress response was meant to propel our bodies into action in the face of acute, short-lived stress. Today, however, humans can be in chronic long-term stress without release. The genetically advantageous mechanism that propelled bodies into action when fleeing from a saber-toothed tiger are now mobilized in the everyday stressors of life. Our challenge then lies in discovering how to continually leverage the stress response to help us thrive and then release it to bring the body back into balance.

Though animals such as dogs intuitively shake their bodies after a stressful moment, humans may have a tendency to hold onto things for a very long time. Emotions can manifest physically as tightness in the abdomen, chest, or throat, and have a physiological effect. Physically discharging stress energy through movement or exercise can help it to move through us. The body and mind hold tension within them until it is released. During the relaxation response, the parasympathetic nervous system is activated to return the body to a state of balance. When my friend and colleague, Clio, asked what she could be doing over winter break to prepare for next semester, my response was to rest, nourish, and recharge. This is some of the most important work we do as teachers so that we can show up clear, open, and grounded.

Our minds and bodies constantly interact and send biofeedback to each other. How our bodies feel can impact mood. Mood can impact the health and posture of our bodies. When we deeply relax, it allows the body a means for letting go and coming back into balance. There are multiple methods of relaxation that are effective for this. Find one that works for you. Some include:

1. Take time to pause and breathe.
2. Meditate to bring awareness to the present moment.
3. Practice restorative yoga to release tension in the body.
4. Spend time in nature to calm the nervous system.
5. Walk without distraction and focus on your breath as you take in your surroundings.
6. Exercise and move your body.
7. Journal about thoughts or experiences to help process events and emotions.
8. Lie down comfortably and listen to relaxing, soothing music or sounds (ocean, forest).

Anxiety

Just as we can learn to work with stress and become better at it, so can we with the umbrella emotion of anxiety. A student in my mindfulness course, Taleen, wrote in a reflection, "I've developed way better methods for dealing with stress and feelings of being overwhelmed. Before I didn't really know how to handle stress-related anxiety, and it would often consume me before I even realized it was happening." Though she still gets anxious and stressed, she now uses meditation as an effective method of facing it head-on. "It's a very easy thing I can do anywhere, without any outside help or tools, that helps me unwind and clear my head."

Surveys from the Introduction to Mindfulness course at USC in the Fall of 2019 indicated that anxiety levels decreased and coping skills increased through the semester as students developed self-awareness tools to manage anxiety. In an initial survey, over half of students remarked they felt anxiety often or very often in a given day. By the end of the semester, this number decreased by half, while being able to cope with anxiety often or very often doubled from 38% to 75%. 83% attributed this much or very much to enrollment in the course.

Though we may not be able to eliminate anxiety, we can change how we view it, learn empowering tools to work with it, and over time lessen the intensity and duration of its effects. "I used to get anxious because of my inability to control the future, and I used to obsessively believe that there was no way to help with my anxiety," reflected mindfulness student, Diego. "After practice I learned that just like how my positive emotions are temporary, so are my negative emotions."

GOBB Technique

The GOBB technique can be useful for times of anxiety to ground, orient and tune into the body and breath. In these times, we can take a moment to get *grounded*. Notice the earth under your feet, your body supported by the surface underneath you. Let your body be held and let it be weighted with gravity. *Orient* yourself to the space around you with your senses. Connect with your *body*. How does it feel? Scan your body from the crown of the head to the soles of your feet, bringing awareness to each part along the way. *Breathe* and notice the breath moving through your body.

GOBB Technique

Ground: get grounded and notice the surface underneath you, your feet supported by the earth.

Orient: orient yourself to the space around you. Tune into your senses to curiously notice what you see, hear, smell, taste, or touch. Note specific objects (red shoes, square tile, blue sky, etc.).

Body: check in with your body to sense how it feels. Where does it feel free or constricted? Scan your body and notice any sensations.

Breath: consciously tune into your breath and take 5–10 deep, slow breaths in and out through the nose.

Each person and situation is different, and I encourage students to find what works for them. Other tips include:

1. Discharge energy with exercise or movement.
2. Use an anchoring phrase like, "May I know that I'm free."
3. Practice the RAIN technique from Chapter 3 (*Recognize* or label emotions, *Allow* them, *Investigate* how they feel in the body, *Non-identify* with them and *nurture* what arises with kindness).
4. Spend time in nature.
5. Journal or draw.
6. Take action to ask, "What's the smallest first step I can take?"
7. Practice self-compassion and hold what arises with kindness.

Classroom Application

A. Ask students what they typically do when they feel stressed out.
B. Ask students to share about a stressful experience. How did they cope with it or how are they coping with it?
C. Take a few deep breaths to pause at the start of class.

Questions for Reflection or Discussion

1. What do you think stress is? What do you think is the opposite of stress?

2. Describe your relationship with stress. What do you usually do when you're stressed out? Discuss a time that you experienced stress. How did you deal with it? What did you learn from it?

3. When might anxiety arise for you? What do you typically do? How does it feel in your body?

4. Activity: Make a list of what's stressing you out. What on the list is in your control? Prioritize those things and make a plan of what you can control and do something about.

C. Application: Self-Care and Self-Compassion

Early on, I had a colleague who would say that teaching is an impossible job. Not in futility, but in recognition that we couldn't possibly do everything the job called for in the conditions, time, and capacity we had. It was an acceptance that allowed her to do her best with the circumstances she had and prioritize time toward what was most important. What is unsustainable won't be sustained. I've seen countless teachers shine bright and burn out. After my second year of teaching, I myself thought I would leave teaching. Ultimately I decided to stay (and nearly twenty years later I'm so glad I did) but I knew I had to make serious adjustments and set boundaries to sustain in the profession. Hollywood glorifies examples of martyr teachers who sacrifice themselves and everything dear to them for their students. What *Freedom Writers* doesn't show you is that she left the classroom after only four years. It is unsustainable to operate intensely for a long duration and maintain work–life balance. So how do we make it sustainable? How can teachers do what they need to do for their students and still honor their own needs? I'm admittedly still a work in progress on this one, but sharing some tips I've found to be helpful along the way:

Simplify
Choose a limited number of things to focus on and do. It is necessary to find ways to reduce items on the plate before adding others on. Sustainable simplicity is most effective when coupled in corresponding levels at the individual, school, district, and state levels. Though it sometimes seems like initiative after initiative waves through education, choosing a focus is necessary for success and sustainability in the field.

Balance Competing Interests
When there are things I need to balance in the classroom—from common assessments, to state tests, to school mandates, to individual needs—my gauge is typically "What is the best thing for my students?" I try to weigh everything and then make my curricular and course decisions based on what is going to be best

for students—in both the short and long term. My yoga teacher, Jeanne, says that the trick about balance isn't about finding it and holding on to it for dear life, it's about finding it, and refinding it, and refinding it. Balance is a continual process, not a final destination.

Pause for Self-Care

Carve time within the day to eat lunch, use the restroom, drink a cup of tea, meditate for a few minutes before class, take a moment to recharge, or whatever you might need. I'm serious. At the very least, I try to take a breath before each class and reset. A short, intentional pause can make a difference in feeling centered and clear. Though the beauty industry seems to have co-opted self-care into consumerism, it is so much more than a facial. Take some time to reflect on what true self-care is for you. What are the things that help you feel restored and refreshed? What does it mean or take for you to unplug from the outside world and plug into yourself? Types of self-care include:

1. *Physical*: do something kind to nourish your body. Workout, walk, cook, eat, move, sleep, dance, or whatever brings you joy.
2. *Emotional*: take time to process and metabolize the emotions that arise through the day. It can be easy to distract or numb emotions, or become overwhelmed by them or explode from them, but instead we can take time to sit with them. Journaling, therapy, and meditation are all useful for me here.
3. *Mental*: do things for mental or intellectual stimulation. Invest time in hobbies, read, go to a museum, or practice gratitude to shift focus.
4. *Social*: connect with friends and family. Make plans to have brunch, send a gratitude text, or play with your pet.
5. *Spiritual*: connect with your inner self and take time to unplug. Meditate, practice yoga, spend time in nature, hike, go to a place of worship, volunteer, or create a morning or evening ritual that is nourishing for you to start or end the day with.

6. *Practical*: Do things that help you feel more organized and clear. Clean, organize, meal prep, get finances in order, make your bed, or whatever it may take for you to feel ready for what's to come.

Admittedly, if we're in survival mode, there is an inherent privilege and luxury in being able to take time or have resources for these things. Please, do not make this another thing to add to the large to-do list or think you need to complete the whole list. It doesn't have to be grand or take a lot of time. Something as simple as a few breaths to pause is a self-care practice I rely on. Keep it simple, meaningful, intentional, and something that can nourish and support you to keep going. For a basic internal assessment, the acronym HALT can be useful here too. When you are *hungry*, eat. When *angry*, journal. When *lonely*, reach out to a friend to make plans. When *tired*, sleep.

Set Boundaries

Boundaries protect our well-being and create safety and clarity around expectations. They communicate what we are willing to do, not do, or put up with. When we are clear on what we want and need, we can sustain in the long term, release resentment, and show up better for ourselves and others. In a district professional development session I facilitated on mindfulness and self-care, teachers went around in a circle naming a self-care they practiced. One participant, said "saying no." When we say no to something, we are saying yes to something else. We are clear on how we want to spend our time and what is important to us. More on this in Chapter 5: Resilience.

Release

A decompression activity can separate the day when leaving work. Going to the gym or a fitness class, taking a walk, listening to a book on tape on the drive home, journaling, or any other separation activity can create a sense of balance and help leave the school day at school.

Get Some Armor

It's not personal. I know that it really felt personal. But it's not. Whether born out of family problems, frustration, systemic design of schooling, issues outside of the classroom, and simply being a young adult, there are countless confounding factors that impact the behavior of students in classroom. The sooner it's realized that there are few things that are directly personal, the sooner we can be more of what students need us to be. This is not to relieve responsibility of professionals to work with what situations have been given to us and show up with our best selves in the classroom, but that the more we can objectively assess situations rather than internalize or personalize them, the more effective the outcome.

Support Networks

Getting to know colleagues can add happiness and mutual support. While teaching is about relationships in the classroom, the relationships outside the classroom have been just as important and nourishing for me to be able to thrive in the profession.

Mindful Self-Compassion

When I ask my students, "How many of you feel like you're too hard on yourselves?" all hands raise. When I ask teachers this question in professional development sessions, they all lift their hands too. Each time. If a friend spoke to us the way we can tend to speak to ourselves, we perhaps would not be their friend. Compassion is when we meet difficulties with kindness. Self-compassion is when we meet our own difficulties, suffering, and challenges with kindness. Over time, we can learn to show ourselves the same kindness that we might give to a friend going through a hard time. Mindful self-compassion involves three elements:

1. *Mindfulness* to recognize that we are experiencing difficulty.
2. *Kindness* in how we relate to ourselves in that moment.

3. *Shared humanity* in recognizing others may have also experienced something similar, or are experiencing something similar.

It can be as simple as pausing, taking a moment, placing a hand to your heart, and sending a phrase of kindness to yourself. Kristen Neff offers the following phrases in her book *Self-Compassion: The Proven Power of Being Kind to Yourself*:

"May I be kind to myself in this moment."
"May I accept this moment exactly as it is."
"May I accept myself in this moment exactly as I am."
"May I give myself all the compassion and courageous action I need."

When discussing self-compassion in class, Philip, asked how he can still motivate himself to get things done if he's being so nice to himself. Self-compassion is not passive or weak. It doesn't mean we don't show up to do what we need to do. It means that we can clearly see what is happening without beating ourselves up about it. We can show up with an energy of wanting what's good and nourishing for ourselves rather than from a place of lack, fear, or not enough. This for me is more motivating and empowering, and makes it so much more enjoyable along the way.

For all the times when we feel like we're not enough, it's important to remember that we are only human, and we do the best we can with who we are at that point in our lives with the circumstances we have. And that's all we can do.

Classroom Application

A. Ask students to raise their hands if they feel like they're too hard on themselves.
B. Practice self-compassion as a class together.
C. Ask students what they do for self-care.

Questions for Reflection or Discussion

1. What does self-care mean to you? What do you do for self-care? What sometimes gets in the way?

2. What do you need in order to make the job sustainable?

3. When might it be useful for you to practice self-compassion?

Bibliography

American College of Health Association. (2019). *National college health assessment spring 2019 reference group executive summary.* Retrieved from https://www.acha.org/documents/ncha/NCHA-II_SPRING_2019_US_REFERENCE_GROUP_EXECUTIVE_SUMMARY.pdf

American Psychological Association. (2013). College students' mental health is a growing concern, survey finds. *American Psychological Association*, *44*(6), 13. https://www.apa.org/monitor/2013/06/college-students

Blackburn, E.H., & Epel, E. (2017). *The telomere effect: A revolutionary approach to living younger, healthier, longer.* New York: Grand Central Publishing.

Brooks, A.W. (2014). Get excited: Reappraising pre-performance anxiety as excitement. *Journal of Experimental Psychology: General 143*(3), 1144–1158. https://www.apa.org/pubs/journals/releases/xge-a0035325.pdf

Gable, S.L., Gonzaga, G.C., & Strachman, A. (2006). Will you be there for me when things go right? Supportive responses to positive event disclosures. *Journal of Personality and Social Psychology*, *91*(5), 904–917. https://doi.org/10.1037/0022-3514.91.5.904

Keller, A., Litzelman, K., Wisk, L.E., Maddox, T., Cheng, E.R., Creswell, P.D., & Witt, W.P. (2012). Does the perception that stress affects health matter? The association with health and mortality. *Health Psychology*, *31*(5), 677–684. https://doi.org/10.1037/a0026743

McGonigal, K. (2015). *The upside of stress: Why stress is good for you, and how to get good at it.* New York: Avery.

National Alliance on Mental Illness. Retrieved from https://www.nami.org

Puddicombe, A. (2012 November). All it takes is 10 mindful minutes. *TED: Ideas Worth Spreading.* Retrieved from https://www.ted.com/talks/andy_puddicombe_all_it_takes_is_10_mindful_minutes

Yaron Weston, L. (2021). *Mindfulness for young adults: Tools to thrive in school and life.* New York: Routledge.

Yaron, L. (2016, July 12). Helping students build mental and physical resiliency. *Education Week.* Retrieved from https://www.edweek.org/tm/articles/2016/07/12/helping-students-build-mental-and-physical-resiliency.html

Yaron, L. (2015, November 11). Mindfulness in the classroom: A how-to guide. *Education Week*. Retrieved from https://www.edweek.org/tm/articles/2015/11/10/mindfulness-in-the-classroom-a-how-to-guide.html

Yaron Weston, L. (2020). Mindfulness in the classroom: Mental health and emotional resilience alongside academic studies. *Liberal Education, Association of American Colleges and Universities, 107*(3), 28–33. https://www.aacu.org/article/mindfulness-in-class-and-in-life-mental-health-and-emotional-resilience-alongside-academic-studies

5

Foundation 5: Resilience

How can I thrive amidst challenge?

FIGURE 5.1

DOI: 10.4324/9781003318408-5

A. Types of Resilience

Resilience is the capacity to thrive amidst challenging circumstances. It is in our nature as humans. We learn to walk by falling and getting back up. Over and over again. Studies show that we can grow resilience. We can look at what gets in the way of it and learn how to bounce back faster and stronger. Like the Japanese art of wabi-sabi, where cracks in broken items are repaired with gold and made even more beautiful, there is a beauty and wisdom in the cracks and difficulties of life and in how we rebuild from them.

Students (and all of us) can learn how to skillfully get back up after falling and view challenges as growth opportunities. Dana, an intelligence and cyber operations major, wrote in a mindfulness course reflection, "My practice has made me a more confident person—confident in my ability to tackle big situations and confident that I am fully 'here' now." Within the curriculum, exploring themes of resilience and overcoming challenges can help students see the resilience of others and reflect on their own capacity to bounce back from challenges. They can explore post-traumatic growth after a difficulty to discover that we are who we are not in spite of, but because of our challenges and how we choose to show up for them. In her memoir, *Know My Name*, Chanel Miller writes, "From grief, confidence has grown, remembering what I've endured. From anger, stemmed purpose. To tuck them away would mean to neglect the most valuable tools this experience has given me." She reflects on her resilience, "I have created a self inside the suffering. Looking back, the assault is not inextricable from the greater story. ... Awful feelings may remain the same, but my capacity to handle them has grown."

There are multiple types of resilience, and different ones are required for different challenges. We might find some easier or more available than others. With a growth mindset, we can learn to grow resilient awareness and responsive action across them. Types of resilience include:

1. *Endurance Resilience*: tenacity, grit, willingness to keep going. When we are tired and want to stop, endurance resilience helps us keep going to take another step.

Discernment is necessary here for a wise endurance so we're not just pushing hard because we're on that track. I grew up as a runner, and endurance is how I was trained. The flip side to endurance is that sometimes I might be so focused on completing the goal that I forget to take a moment and pause and listen inwards to discern if I should be enduring or if I should find another route. When I ran the LA marathon, I decided I was going to do it nonstop. And I did. Even through a cramp in my quad the last few miles. And so many years later, I still feel a slight pull in my knee reminding me of the wisdom of pausing to ask, "Is it wise for me to keep going like this?"

2. *Adaptability Resilience*: capacity to change and adapt to circumstances. What do we do when something isn't as expected? How do we pivot to a new direction and to what extent do we accept or resist change? My colleague and friend, Kristin, and I repeatedly have cause to remark that change is the only constant in schooling (and life). We get comfortable with how things are, and they inevitably change. Some change is voluntary, some is chosen for us. Some is gradual and gives us time to prepare, while other changes are sudden. Some we welcome, and others we resist. Psychologist and mindfulness teacher Chris Germer offers the equation: pain x resistance = suffering. Pain is inevitable in life. The amount we suffer depends on our ability to accept what is happening and adapt to circumstances as they arise.

3. *Emotional Resilience*: navigate difficult emotions; emotional intelligence. How do we navigate, process, and metabolize the emotions that arise in our human experience? Though sometimes emotions may overwhelm us or other times we may want to push emotions away and ignore them, emotional resilience is the wisdom to recognize emotions and skillfully process them. The mindfulness technique RAIN can be helpful for building this skill (*Recognize* or label emotions, *Allow* them, *Investigate* how they feel in the body, *Non-identify* with them and *nurture* what arises with kindness). The way of the world is to

take things in and let things go. We inhale oxygen, and exhale carbon dioxide. We eat food, absorb nutrients, and eliminate the waste. In either situation, it wouldn't be wise to hold it in or push away. Same with emotions. We can learn to trust that we can take a breath through an emotion and navigate it the best we can.

4. *Resilience to Learn from Challenges*: fall down and get up stronger. When we fall short or make a mistake, how do we view it and us? Along the way, we may learn to fear failure, or have failed so many times we stop trying, or learn helplessness when we don't feel any agency in a situation. Learning to view challenges with a growth mindset can cultivate even greater growth through embracing the learning process of life. We can identify what gets in the way of this growth and remind ourselves that we have what it takes to do our best.

5. *Resourcefulness Resilience*: find a way. When one door closes, find another. Things often (rarely) go as planned. What do we do then? How do we find what we need in order to thrive in a situation that perhaps isn't planned or ideal? This capacity for problem solving, creativity, and critical thinking allows us to create and embrace an option b, and maybe even have it work out better than the original plan. It's not what happens, but what we do with what happens that makes us resourceful and successful. In times when the next option isn't clear, it can be helpful to talk it through with others, journal, go for a walk to get some space from it, and ask, "What do I have? What do I need?" There is a power in the acceptance that things are as they are. Acceptance isn't passive—it's a clear seeing that can lead to wise action.

6. *Resilience from Loss*: coping with loss and grief. No one is exempt. My teacher Matthew says there are only those who have grieved and those who will grieve. We will all suffer loss in life. Loss of what and those we love, loss of relationships, loss of jobs, loss of the health of our bodies. When I lost my mom to cancer, it was devastating. My

mindfulness practice allowed me to openheartedly show up for her in her last months, and to process the grief after. It still comes in waves but over time has softened around the edges as I leaned into acceptance, gratitude, the truth of impermanence, and holding close the relationships I have. My dad, in his mid-eighties now, never learned to cope with his emotions. He is used to being tough and stuffing them down, and so when faced with all the guilt and loneliness, he's had so much difficulty bouncing back, and after four years is in a state of prolonged intense grief. He has such strong endurance resilience, but when faced with such loss, he hasn't yet found the pathway out. We are all just doing our best, and it's so hard, and at the same time, we can learn to extract the good and carry on. I know, easier said than done, but we have to try. What's the alternative?

7. *Interpersonal Resilience*: building resilient and lasting relationships. Connection to others is hardwired into what it means to be human. And there are also things we can do to build and sustain relationships. It's not just how often we connect with someone or for how long, but openness and vulnerability that can deepen a friendship. How do we show that we care for others? How do we check in, listen, be there for them—both in times of need and in times of joy? Research shows that how we celebrate good news can have an impact on relationships. One study categorized responses to hearing someone else's good news into four types: active constructive (expressing enthusiasm and interest, asking questions), passive constructive (simple validation of "good job," no enthusiasm or follow-up questions), active destructive (concern or negative response), passive destructive (ignores news). Of the types of responses, active constructive responses to good news increased connection in friendships. I tell my students about this study and invite them to practice sharing and responding to good news in pairs.

8. *Resilience of the Heart*: the capacity of the heart to heal and stay open. For all that the heart has to bear, it can develop

defense mechanisms and armor to protect itself. It might shut down or fear opening up to another person again after a heartache. Living a wholehearted life means learning how to open and reopen the heart amidst the wounds it acquires. An important element of this is forgiveness and how we learn to forgive others and forgive ourselves. Forgiveness isn't condoning behavior—it's an acceptance of what happened that releases the power and grip that person or experience has over us. Forgiveness isn't about the other person as much as it is about ourselves finding freedom to let go of resentment. In the mindfulness practice of forgiveness, the following phrases can be repeated silently in meditation:

"May I forgive myself/you for making mistakes."
"May I accept that I am/you are a learner still learning life's lessons."
"May I forgive myself/you for the harm I/you have done, knowingly or unknowingly."
"And if I cannot forgive myself/you now, may I do so sometime in the future."

9. *Goal Resilience:* the persistence of what it takes to see a goal through. This often means delayed gratification, impulse control, planning, and the awareness of who we are and what we need in order to keep going. Willpower is supported by the purpose in knowing that what we invest will be worth it on the other side. It has to be important enough, and we have to believe it's possible enough to persist through the challenges that arise along the way. Some will undoubtedly have more challenges and less support in reaching goals. It is a simplification to imply impulse control and willpower are gatekeepers to goals without discussing the social factors that contribute to them. And at the same time, it is also possible to learn how to get better at goal resilience in the face of challenges.

10. *Hope Resilience:* sustaining the belief in something good to come. In the times when things are tough and we don't see the light, hope can keep us going in the resilience of perspective to believe. In an interview, football coach Pete

Carroll said, "I live my life thinking something good is just about to happen to me." Hope is contagious. When we are hopeful, others may feel more hopeful too. This is not to say we need to be delusional, but to keep open the door for the possibility of good. When we think we can do something, we have a far better chance of doing it than if we don't believe. Taken from another football coach, Ted Lasso, I put up a yellow BELIEVE sign in my office.

Foundations of Success

Early on, it was clear that in the same classroom some students thrived, and others didn't. The answer is complex, with factors of socioeconomic status, parental involvement, relationships with caring adults, expectations, access, resources, equity, conditions of schooling, mentoring, luck, and countless others contributing to success. Even amidst systemic inequities, what are the individual mindsets that make some students more likely to succeed than others? I noticed students who exhibited the following strengths seemed to have a higher likelihood of success:

◆ *Purpose* in why they were there and what they wanted to do in their lives. They set goals to drive that purpose, and priorities to help them delay gratification and keep the big picture in mind. They organized their time and calendar around their goals. They felt like they mattered, and what they did mattered, and that they could make a difference beyond themselves.

◆ *Endurance resilience* to keep going when things got difficult. They were willing to do more and go farther. I used to ask students, "What do you do when things get difficult?" Their character and opportunities are defined in these times.

◆ *Adaptability* in being able to accept change and adapt to circumstances, and a growth mindset to learn from challenges.

◆ *Positive relationships* with caring adults. This includes seeking out and being open to the relationship.

◆ *Resourcefulness* to find what they need when it isn't readily or easily available.

While seemingly inherent, these attributes are teachable, train-able, and necessary for student success. Ben, a political economy major, wrote in a mindfulness course reflection, "I feel more in touch with the people around me, more appreciative of the life that I live, and also much more alive and ready for whatever challenges I may face." These elements can be integrated into curricular themes where individuals in history and literature can be explicitly studied and tracked for them, and students can do self-studies of their own strengths and next steps in building them. This is not to put an achievement ideology on students and relieve the system of responsibility for becoming more equi-table so they wouldn't have to be so resilient in the first place, but to say that there are things we can do to make success more likely even amidst challenging circumstances.

A firefighter was a classroom guest speaker for my freshman thematic unit Decision Making in Times of Crisis. He challenged students to think about where they lived. He said that some people lived in the problem, while others lived in the solution. Living in the solution means recognizing the challenges that exist and creating actionable solutions within available means. Teaching an explicitly empowering curriculum of resilience trains students to live in the solution by recognizing their own patterns and helping them develop tools to overcome challenges. As a teacher the classroom, this can look like:

Leading with Strengths

Leveraging strengths in the classroom can create a more effective and aligned learning experience. This can be used in curriculum planning, delivery, and relationship building. Perhaps a student who is an artist can design the cover for a class poetry book, or another who is skilled in technology can manage a class web-site. Knowing the strengths of students can engage them in the learning process and show them that what they have to offer is important and unique to the class. As a teacher, I know that a strength I have is building relationships in one-on-one interac-tions, and so I structure that time in—whether through greeting them as they arrive in class, check-in discussions, or following up on what they are going through.

Adjusting the Stimulus to Get the Response You Want

When I was student teaching at the start of my career, a group of students sat at a round table at the side of the room and talked to each other throughout class. The next day, my guiding teacher, Heidi, placed a pile of books on the table so that they couldn't sit there. She disrupted the space associated with the undesirable behavior so she could gain the response she wanted. This showed me the power of adjusting the stimulus to get a different response. What is the lever to create a desired change and redirect the response?

If It's Not Working, Change It

Teaching is a constant reflection of what's working, what's not, and how to make it even better. It is important to design and implement structures that support student learning in a positive classroom culture. Be vigilant as to how those structures are working and adjust when needed. I might leverage a new start, such as a new month, week, or curricular unit/module, as a time to reset. I tell them why we're changing directions, redirect attention to classroom norms or reset norms, and then monitor vigilantly to be sure that what I am resetting is enforced and followed.

Classroom Application

A. Ask students to write and share their resilience stories of a time that was both challenging and a source of meaning or growth. How did they cope with it? What did they learn? How did it change them?

B. Study stories, themes, or curricular units of individuals who overcame challenges.

C. Ask students to interview someone about a challenge they overcame, how they overcame it, and what lessons they learned from it.

D. Ask students to identify which of the ten types of resilience they feel strongest in and which are next step areas for them.

Questions for Reflection or Discussion

1. What is your resilience story? Share about a time that was challenging and a source of meaning and growth. How did you deal with it? What did it teach you? How did it change you?

2. Which of the ten resilience types are easiest or hardest for you at this point?

3. What does it mean and take for you to live in the solution as an educator?

B. Relentless Sparkle

Some people are shinier than others. They seem to have discovered some secret that enables them to live a little lighter no matter the weight of the world, to find goodness in each challenge, to spaciously open their minds and hearts even after being hurt. They shine and sparkle relentlessly, and seemingly effortlessly. I know, I hate those people too.

But we can all learn to tap into our inner shine—and leverage positive psychology research to help us. Psychologist Martin Seligman's PERMA theory of well-being includes five building blocks of flourishing: **P**ositive emotion, **E**ngagement, **R**elationships, **M**eaning, and **A**ccomplishment. They can be enhanced through practices like cultivating gratitude and hope, finding flow and engagement in activities, building connections with others, discovering purpose in something bigger than ourselves, and pursuing accomplishments that we can take pride in. This is not to remove responsibility from schools—there are certainly things schools can do to make it easier for people in them to sparkle so they don't have to work so hard and overcome so much to do it.

We can learn to savor the moments of our lives and savor joy. Sometimes in a great learning or life moment, I'll pause to take it in and acknowledge it. We can learn to share and receive joy with others too. Students enjoy the activity of sharing three good things with each other or sharing good news.

We can also train our minds to be more fully present. A Harvard study found that people's minds wandered about half the time—and they were less happy when their minds were wandering, no matter what they were doing. It makes sense. We could be on a beautiful island, but if we're too stuck in our minds in the past of what happened, or too focused on what might happen that we don't enjoy where we are, we'd be less happy than if we were in an ordinary place, content in the present moment. In a flow state, we're in the zone and fully immersed in an activity. Good moments of teaching are like this for me, as are art, writing, yoga, a rich conversation with a friend—activities where I need to bring my whole self in. Named by psychologist Mihály Csíkszentmihályi in 1975, flow is an energizing, full involvement and absorption of self where we aren't thinking about the past or the future, but immersed in the moment.

Relationships are essential too. Particularly when we practice vulnerability, empathy, and compassion in them. Though we may think of it as helping others, we ourselves greatly benefit from generosity and altruism, as we also do from expressing gratitude. Writing a gratitude text and letter are part of my curriculum. When a student said his mom got worried after receiving his gratitude text, I joked that perhaps we should be expressing gratitude more often.

Technology

Technology is neither good nor bad—it's how we use it and our relationship to it that makes the difference. It has the capacity to build knowledge, entertainment, and connection, and also at the same time can dim our sparkle by unconscious, habitual use. Mindful awareness of technology use gives us power over how we use devices and how we can purposefully choose to use our time. I ask students in my mindfulness course to reflect on what it means to manage their devices so their devices aren't managing them. We have a mostly tech-free classroom, with purposeful technology use on occasion. I tell students about studies that have found that retention of information is worse for those taking notes on their laptops—for them and those around them—and ask them why that might be. I pose exploratory questions like, "Does technology further or hinder connection?" We talk about how phones are designed to be maximally appealing to keep our attention, and discuss the power and freedom of consciously choosing where to place our attention. Norms for purposeful use of technology in the classroom can elevate learning and contribute to the discussion of what it means to live and learn in the age of technology.

Like many other students, Danika used to walk with a phone in hand, oblivious to her surroundings. "I would anxiously walk on campus while glued to my phone with my air pods in; however, recently I have been more proactive about putting my phone away and simply enjoying my surroundings." She noticed a difference in her mindset and how she related to the world around her. "Listening to the sounds of nature and looking at the scenery around me is an incredibly refreshing experience that makes me feel much more calm, grounded, and present." Similarly, other students who apply mindfulness to technology use in their group choice projects try strategies like not having phones out while eating, sleeping with the phone in another room, powering down well before going to bed, monitoring screen time, deleting apps, and noting a reason for going on their phone before doing so. They save hours a day that are then spent on things that are more aligned with goals, happiness, or real-world connection. Technology use evolves. Though my students are way more connected to technology than I was at their age, they remark at how shocked they are that the younger generation is so much more connected than they were at their age. What will this mean for their growing physical bodies, friendships, community sports programs, play, and so many more facets of youth that are being redefined?

Signature Strengths

Each of us has unique strengths and talents. No one of us has all the talents. No one of us is absent of talents. No one of us alone is stronger than all of us together. How do we learn to nurture these gifts and embrace the uniqueness? How do we teach students to recognize and grow them? The Values in Action (VIA) Classification lists 24 character strengths grouped into six core virtues:

- ◆ *Wisdom*: creativity, curiosity, judgment, love of learning, perspective
- ◆ *Courage*: bravery, perseverance, honesty, zest
- ◆ *Humanity*: love, kindness, social intelligence
- ◆ *Justice*: teamwork, fairness, leadership
- ◆ *Temperance*: forgiveness, humility, prudence, self-regulation
- ◆ *Transcendence*: appreciation of beauty and excellence, gratitude, hope, humor, spirituality

A character strengths survey is available free online at www.viacharacter.org to better understand which are prominent for you personally. This could be something useful to try with students when discussing college and careers.

Self-reflection is the heart of learning. Samuel, my former high school student who went on to graduate college and become a psychologist, reflected, "I believe that in order to achieve academic success, students must be able to analyze and understand their own behaviors, tendencies, and habits in respect to their own learning process." He found this introspection and reflection essential to performance and engagement. "Though academic success may be perceived differently among individuals, it still requires learning how to manage one's social and physical environment and time, as well figure out which learning strategies work best for them for each of their individual classes."

While some people may seem born shiny, it takes effort and relentless vigilance to sparkle and stay in tune with what we need and who we are. Though we may have a set happiness range, there are certainly things we and our students can do within that range that will make a difference in our capacity to flourish.

Time Affluence

With all there is to do as a teacher, there often just doesn't seem to be enough time. And while we can't insert more hours in the day, we can reframe our relationship with time toward one of affluence, rather than scarcity. Time famine is framing our experience as "There isn't enough time." Time affluence implies that there is plenty of time. Instead of *only* having an hour to teach a classroom lesson, we have a *whole* hour to teach a lesson. Instead of rushing around tiring ourselves out trying to get things done, we can simplify and identify what isn't important and where the gold really lies.

So much of our time is spent planning for the future or reflecting on the past. A component of time affluence is to allow ourselves the freedom and luxury of being in the present moment. We can learn to prioritize our time around the things that are the most important and redefine our relationship with time. A part of this is identifying what might be getting in the way. Known as the Zeigarnik effect, the mind has a tendency to be drawn to unfinished tasks. My mind will turn over an upcoming task, trying to find the most efficient or optimum path. Things I've found helpful for releasing the grip are making a list of what I need to do, completing a quick unfinished task, or visualizing a red checkmark on an imaginary file folder of the task. That way the mind doesn't have to hold it so tightly.

It is not so simple when we have countless things to do as a teacher and the stakes are so high. And yet, we can learn to simplify what is important and reframe and reclaim our relationship with time.

Boundaries

Particularly in a profession that asks so much, and keeps asking for even more, setting boundaries is necessary to sustain as a teacher. It can be easy to say yes to it all, because all of it is so important, but when we say yes to something, it means we're saying no to something else. When I say yes to an extra committee, it means I'm saying no whatever else I might have done with that time. This opportunity cost might be too high when the little yeses add up. Both in and out of the classroom, it's important to set boundaries, communicate them, and reinforce them. What am I willing to do? What do I want to do? What brings me joy? When I'm saying yes to _____, do I feel it as a lowercase *yes* or a capital, bold **YES**, and how does that resonate for me?

Nedra Glover Tawwab's book *Set Boundaries: Find Peace* explores three types of boundaries: porous, meaning that they are loose and don't communicate or follow through on what we need. Rigid, meaning they are strict in what we want from others with no room for flexibility. Or healthy boundaries, where we communicate what we need and back it up with action. For healthy boundaries, we need to be aware of what we need, communicate that clearly, and enforce it. Boundaries exist across all relationships in our lives. And, it's not just with others. Setting boundaries with ourselves is just as important. How much time am I willing to spend on work this weekend? Whether our relationships with technology, food, finances, or any other countless things we turn attention to, we can reclaim our lives by bringing awareness, being intentional about what is good and nourishing for us, and making choices aligned with our priorities.

Classroom Application

A. Invite students to take the character strengths survey at www.viacharacter.org. Which are they strongest in? How do/might they show up in their lives?

B. Ask students to explore their relationship with technology and set technology goals.

C. Ask students when they are most often in a state of flow. When are they most present? Least present?

D. What do healthy boundaries and time affluence in the classroom look like to you?

Questions for Reflection or Discussion

1. What are the things that make you sparkle? What are the things that dim your sparkle?

2. What are your most prominent signature strengths? How might they be leveraged in the classroom?

3. When do you feel time famine? What might it take for you to experience time affluence?

4. What is your dominant boundary style (porous, rigid, healthy)? What is the benefit and the cost? What is a next step for you with boundaries?

C. Application: Leading Positive Change

When I started out teaching, my mentor told me that we each have a drop of impact that we have control over. We may not be able to control what's outside of that drop, but that drop is ours. In the moments when it seems like the system is too big to shift, I try to pause and zero in on what is in my drop and what I can do within it. Each drop collectively can create a river of change. In this is a resilience to work toward a positive, actionable shift in education.

A singular teacher will not be able to sustainably meet all the needs of a child, yet together working with a team of individuals, with support from the top, it is possible to make a significant difference. To leverage school-wide change, building relationships with colleagues and the community is just as important as building relationships with students. Incrementally working toward sustainable, collaborative, and systemic solutions can expand what is in a teacher's drop of impact. Identifying entry points for change, early wins, and win–win alternatives can all start the process. Over time, I've come to find that for my voice and message to be heard, I need to speak in the language of those who are making the decisions. This includes:

- ◆ *Building relationships*: taking the time to care about and build genuine relationships with key decision-makers and those around them.
- ◆ *Doing the homework*: exploring information about the issue locally to identify best practices. This can help identify possible entry points for change. I found that it was more effective to show an entry point rather than assume it would be found.
- ◆ *Seeking mutual interests*: identify what is important to the person you're talking to and how it connects to your interest and needs. Make it a win-win.
- ◆ *Telling personal stories*: the stories of educators and students humanize what is happening in schools. Find a short personal story that addresses your issue and be clear about the message you want to communicate.

◆ *Being clear about your ask*: perhaps give a few options so that the individual you are asking has some choice and flexibility. At the very least, an invitation to your classroom or school can be a first step.

◆ *Following up and following through*: build credibility with next steps to establish a long-term, reciprocal relationship.

Implementation

The effectiveness of an initiative depends on how it is implemented, who is involved in the process, and what supports there are to positively shift change toward it. In a classroom, school, and district, strategic implementation of smart, aligned policy is a key to success. With vigilance and reflection, there should be care and thought into what happens before, during, and after a change. This includes being intentional about implementation plans, particularly with the countless changes sweeping through schools that seem to add to existing plans and full plates, rather than replace or consolidate. Helpful guiding questions for creating school change:

1. Why is this plan important?
2. Who needs to be involved? In what capacity and at what stages?
3. What will it take to enact the plan?
4. What are the benchmarks for progress? How long will each take?
5. Do people believe in or want this plan?
6. What will the plan replace?
7. How do people feel about the plan? How can we measure this periodically?
8. What professional development is needed?
9. How will we know we're successful?

Pre-Change

Before a new initiative in a classroom, school or district, there should be an exploration of the existence and effectiveness of current processes. Are there existing best practices to draw from? What data, research, or evidence is needed to understand the situation? For investment and ownership, key stakeholders, including teachers, students, parents, and community leaders, should be partners in the process. Affording staff, students, families, and community members clear, specific roles helps make sure the change is happening *with* them, not *to* them. Processes should be instituted to make decisions about how change will occur.

The 5W's are a helpful framework here:

♦ *What* is the goal/vision? How should it be established and communicated?

♦ *Who* will accomplish it? Who's at the table in creating the plan and making decisions?

♦ *What* are the deliverables? What are the levers and entry points? How much time, effort, and funding might it take? What are the challenges that may arise?

♦ *When* is the timeline? Is this an ongoing, sustainable process, or a one-time event?

♦ *Where* will collaboration take place?

♦ *Why*: What is the purpose of this change? What are the mutual interests?

Exploration of these questions is important for transparency and clarity of a roadmap to know what is being accomplished, when and how it will be accomplished, and the role of those involved. This all may seem like a lot of effort to go through when a unilateral decision can just be made, but process is essential to effective implementation.

During Change

Implement with careful attention to the end goal and components necessary to achieve it. Appropriate time and support to reach the goal can make or break the initiative. Solicit feedback and address feelings and hesitancies about the change. Is there support from the top and investment from within, and what might it take to gain or sustain that support?

Collect data along the way to show impact and make it visible and aligned with mutual interests. My second semester into teaching the mindfulness course I developed, I collected pre- and post-surveys from students to measure impact. I was able to draw on that data and show in a tangible, measurable way the impact the program was having on student lives and academics. I wrote articles on it and students shared their experiences in panel discussions. This visibility left no doubt about the impact the program was having, and allowed us to be able to grow the program with support from leadership.

Be mindful of culture throughout the process. Change brings up a lot of fear, and with it a tremendous opportunity to work through it collectively. As we were preparing to initiate a school-wide observation process at my high school, staff listed their hopes and fears, as well as created guidelines for what they were and were not okay with when observers came to their classrooms. This seemed to create more ease knowing that feelings were valid and valued and that classroom space would be respected.

Post-Change

Change is hard work. As humans, it is in our nature to want to see the impact of our efforts. Particularly in the beginning to generate momentum, as well as throughout the process, it is important to show how that policy made a difference for students, staff, classes, and schools. The more concrete these data, the more it will create a desire to keep going forward. Whether pre-/post-assessment data, impact survey reflections, testimonials, or student achievement information, showing value can help sustain investment. After a change has been implemented, there should be regular checks to ensure the change is well received. How will we know if it was successful or what impact it had? What are lessons learned and takeaways that might be helpful for future collaborations? To what extent did the goal/vision align with the process and outcomes of the collaboration? What are the next steps?

Surveying change recipients and regular check-ins can help ensure that the implementation is meaningful and sticks. Feedback collection throughout the process can help keep a pulse on how people are feeling and the culture that is developing as a byproduct of those feelings, so that the leadership team can flexibly modify plans as needed.

Professional Development

In addition to grading tall stacks of papers, attending professional development meetings might be one of the most dreaded parts of the job. What makes it that much more aggravating is that it doesn't have to be. In response to an article I wrote about how to have quality professional development, a former assistant principal (who likely led much PD himself) said it was an oxymoron. I disagree and say that it's possible. And that it takes thoughtfulness in doing something different than what is traditionally done.

Years ago, a colleague sat in on a professional development meeting where we discussed the needs of students and teachers and how to best spend program money in alignment with those needs. After he left, he said it was a good discussion, but it wasn't really PD. He was right. I've seen the range of PD through my career and know it's absolutely possible to create meaningful spaces for educators to dialogue, grow, and apply what they learn to the classroom. This doesn't happen in PD that is a one-time dissemination of information that could have been emailed, drive-bys of disconnected workshops, retelling what's already known, meeting for the sake of meeting, disconnected from classroom realities, or delivered via death by PowerPoint. Good PD happens with, not to, teachers. It values the professional expertise and leadership of educators. It isn't passively received, but it is interacted with and created through meaningful engagement. It is part of a continuum that connects to a larger vision of how the school and district can better meet the needs of students and teachers. It creates the space and time for authentic collaboration.

Quality PD also involves considering the 5W's:

1. *Who* is included in the planning, execution, and follow-up to be sure PD is grounded in the realities of the classroom and builds faculty ownership?
2. *What* learning experience will occur and what supports might teachers need for classroom implementation?
3. *When* will smaller and larger goals be achieved, and how will we know if we have achieved what we set out to?

4. *Where* is the best space to encourage collaboration and in what configuration is that space, whether small group, whole group, or even off campus with community organizations?
5. *Why* are participants in this particular PD?

When building PD structures, it can be helpful to create shared norms, set an intention, monitor equity in voice and decision making, and take a few moments to pause and breathe when coming together in the busyness of the school day.

As the Lead Mindfulness Teacher in our department, I create PD for our team, many for whom this is their first experience as classroom teachers and they have not attended a classroom teacher training program. After a meeting, one of our new teachers asked me, "Can we do more of that?" Seriously. We share facilitation around a topic that is often raised earlier in the semester or at the previous meeting. For example, one colleague brought up wanting to learn more about how to expand diversity, equity, and inclusion in her classroom. This was our 40-minute meeting structure:

Opening few moments to breathe (facilitator 1)
Inquiry question: What does it mean for you to be a teacher who (racially/ethnically/culturally) identifies as _____? (facilitator 2)
Best practices sharing and collaboration: What does diversity, equity, inclusion mean to you and what might it look like in the/your classroom? (facilitator 3)
Closing breath (facilitator 4)

As a next step, or if we built in more time, we would have a space for curriculum/instructional application. Since we meet three times over the semester, it's an ongoing dialogue across curriculum, instruction, and inquiry. As a next step, we are now transitioning to rotating meeting point people, so each team member has the chance to choose the topics and discussion questions for meetings.

My most impactful professional development has been outside of school walls. Quality teacher programs have invigorated my teaching, broadened my perspective, and built my capacity as a teacher leader—while traveling and meeting other incredible teachers at the same time. Here are a few I've loved:

- ◆ U.S. Department of Education School Ambassador Fellowship: engage in the creation, evaluation, and dissemination of information around national education initiatives.
- ◆ Fulbright-Hayes Seminars Abroad Project: travel seminars for educators to improve their understanding and knowledge of the peoples and cultures of other countries.
- ◆ Teachers for Global Classrooms Program: training, experience abroad, and global collaboration to apply an international perspective to the classroom.
- ◆ Teach Plus Fellowship: learn about education policy and advocacy. Work to improve laws and policies at the school, district, and state levels.
- ◆ National Endowment for the Humanities (NEH): summer residential programs to study a variety of humanities topics.

School Application

A. Explore how change is typically approached in your school.
B. Reflect on what professional development looks like in your school. To what extent are the 5W's considered in the planning and execution? Which might be most useful?
C. What's an area you'd like to explore or grow as a teaching professional?

Questions for Reflection or Discussion

1. What does creating positive change mean or look like to you?

2. What processes for teacher and student leadership exist in your school and community?

3. What do you think is needed for effective implementation of a program or initiative at your school site?

D. Conclusion

At the end of her first semester as a classroom teacher, I asked my colleague, JoAnna, how it went. She replied, "You set me up for success." What does it mean to set our students up for success? What does it take for schools to set teachers up for success? What are the conditions needed for our classrooms, schools, and communities to thrive?

Even after all these years, there are perhaps more questions than answers. What does it mean to really care for our students? What does it take? How can we magnify student voices and leadership? How can we magnify teacher voices and leadership? How can we elevate the teaching profession? How can schools become places of well-being and sustainability where those in them can flourish? What will it take to create equitable school structures that align well-being supports alongside academic studies? If systems function the way they are designed to function, what is the design of schools that can humanize, engage, uplift, and inspire? More than fixed answers, we can live in these questions and strive toward more equitable and caring spaces for teachers and students.

On a fieldtrip to a UCLA music performance, the musician asked students what sound their life made. With the echo of so many sounds in education, it is important to be deliberate about what sound we want our classrooms, schools, and communities to make. From here we can intentionally identify the necessary elements, instruments, and conditions that will create those sounds. With that in mind, I am reminded what an honor it is to be in this business of changing lives and magnifying those sounds of opportunity and hope.

Bibliography

Baumeister, R., & Tierney, J. (2011). *Willpower: Rediscovering the greatest human strength*. New York: Penguin.

Bryant, F.B., & Veroff, J. (2007). *Savoring: A new model of positive experience*. Mahwah: Lawrence Erlbaum Associates.

Contrepois, K., Wu, S., Moneghetti, K.J., Hornburg, D., Ahadi, S., Tsai, M.S., ... Snyder, M.P. (2020). Molecular choreography of acute exercise. *Cell, 181*(5), 1112–1130. https://doi.org/10.1016/j.cell.2020.04.043

Cuddy, A. (2012 June). Your body language may shape who you are. *TED: Ideas Worth Spreading*. Retrieved from https://www.ted.com/talks/amy_cuddy_your_body_language_may_shape_who_you_are

Cuddy, A. (2016). *Presence: Bringing your boldest self to your biggest challenges*. New York: Little, Brown and Company, Hachette Book Company.

Csikszentmihalyi, M. (1990). *Flow: The psychology of optimal experience*. New York: Harper & Row.

Dietary Guidelines Advisory Committee. (2015–2020). *Dietary guidelines report*. Retrieved from https://health.gov/our-work/food-nutrition/2015-2020-dietary-guidelines

Duckworth, A. (2016). *Grit: The power of passion and perseverance*. New York: Scribner.

Duhigg, C. (2012). *The power of habit: Why we do what we do in life and business*. New York: Random House.

Dynarsky, S. (2017 August 10). For better learning in college lectures, lay down the laptop and pick up the pen. *Brookings*. Retrieved from https://www.brookings.edu/research/for-better-learning-in-college-lectures-lay-down-the-laptop-and-pick-up-a-pen/

Ellenbogen, J.M., Hu, P.T., Payne, J.D., Titone, D., & Walker, M.P. (2007). Human relational memory requires time and sleep. *Proceedings of the National Academy of Sciences University of the Sunshine Coast, 104*(18), 7723–7728. https://doi.org/10.1073/pnas.0700094104

Gable, S.L., Gonzaga, G.C., & Strachman, A. (2006). Will you be there for me when things go right? Supportive responses to positive event disclosures. *Journal of Personality and Social Psychology, 91*(5), 904–917. https://doi.org/10.1037/0022-3514.91.5.904

Gerbarg, P. (2016, November 30). Neurobiology and neurophysiology of breath practices in psychiatric care. *Psychiatric Times, 33*, 22. http://doi.org/10.1016/j.psc.2013.01.001

Korb, A. (2015). *The upward spiral: Using neuroscience to reverse the course of depression, one small change at a time.* Oakland, CA: New Harbinger Publications.

Locke, E.A., & Latham, G.P. (2002). Building a practically useful theory of goal setting and task motivation: A 35-year odyssey. *American Psychologist, 57*(9), 705–717. https://doi.org/10.1037/0003-066X.57.9.705

Lyubomirsky, S., Sheldon, K.M., & Schkade, D. (2005). Pursuing happiness: The architecture of sustainable change. *Review of General Psychology, 9*(2), 111–131. https://doi.org/10.1037/1089-2680.9.2.111

Lyubomirsky, S. (2007). *The how of happiness: A new approach to getting the life you want.* New York: Penguin Books.

McGonigal, K. (2011). *The willpower instinct.* New York: Penguin Publishing Group.

Miller, C. (2019). *Know my name: A memoir.* New York: Viking.

Seligman, M. (2012). *Flourish: A visionary new understanding of happiness and well- being.* New York: Atria Books.

Tawwab, N.G. (2021). *Set boundaries, find peace: A guide to reclaiming yourself.* New York: Penguin Random House.

Yaron, L. (2017). The Five Ws of Quality Professional Development. *Ed Week.* http://www.edweek.org/tm/articles/2017/05/09/the-five-ws-of-quality-professional-development.html

Zeigarnik, B. (1938). On finished and unfinished tasks. In W.D. Ellis (Ed.), *A source book of Gestalt psychology* (pp. 300–314). London: Kegan Paul, Trench, Trubner & Company.

Appendix A

Sample Curricular Units and Syllabus

The following are some of my favorite units. They are interdisciplinary and multi-genre, situated in historical context. Suggested grade levels are listed, though they can be modified to fit across grade levels. For variety, more options for suggested texts are included than are detailed in the curricular unit plans. Like anything here, take what works, leave behind the rest, and modify to fit your needs and style.

Thematic Unit 1: Here I Stand (Grades 11–12)

Unit Summary

Students will explore how individuals in literature, history, and life stand up for their beliefs, the methods by which they stand for them, and the costs and benefits of choosing a position to stand for. Students will examine their own belief systems and stances, and will complete a culminating project in which they will portray what, how, and why they stand for what they do. Through the unit, students will build skills in reading, writing, speaking, and listening, in a critical thinking, solutions-based, global competence framework.

Common Core State Standards

1. CCSS.ELA-LITERACY.RI.11-12.1. Cite strong and thorough textual evidence to support analysis of what the text says explicitly as well as inferences drawn from the text, including determining where the text leaves matters uncertain.
2. CCSS.ELA-LITERACY.W.11-12.1. Write arguments to support claims in an analysis of substantive topics or texts, using valid reasoning and relevant and sufficient evidence.

3. CCSS.ELA-LITERACY.SL.11-12.1. Initiate and participate effectively in a range of collaborative discussions (one-on-one, in groups, and teacher-led) with diverse partners on grades 11–12 topics, texts, and issues, building on others' ideas and expressing their own clearly and persuasively.

Possible Texts

◆ *NPR This I Believe* "When Ordinary People do Extraordinary Things," Jody Williams
◆ "Letter from a Birmingham City Jail," Martin Luther King, Jr.
◆ *Bhagavad Gita*
◆ *Antigone*, Sophocles
◆ *Night*, Elie Wiesel
◆ *The Apology*, Plato
◆ *The Kite Runner*, Khaled Housseini
◆ *A Doll's House*, Henrik Ibsen
◆ *Between the World and Me*, Ta-Nehisi Coates
◆ *Invisible Women*, Caroline Criado Perez
◆ Speech: *Perils of Indifference*, Elie Wiesel
◆ Song: "Where is the Love?," Black Eyed Peas
◆ Film: *Promising Young Woman*
◆ Art: *Guernica*, Picasso
◆ Historical Connection: educational equity, civil rights movement, environment

Thematic Vocabulary
conviction, principle, allegiance, loyalty, adherence, obligation, conscientious, constancy, conflicting, contradictory, conformity, autonomy

Summative Assessments

1. *Essay*: Using at least three of the texts studied this unit, analyze the causes and results of conflicting allegiances as they apply to global or generational cultural constructs.

Include: what the individuals stand for, why they make the decisions they do, what factors enable their success or failure, and discuss the broader implications of their actions.

2. *Here I Stand* Project: Create a written statement and visual representation of what you stand for and the challenges that you've overcome to get to where you are. Present in a class showcase.

Sample Learning Questions and Activities on Select Texts

Difference and Indifference

Text: "When Ordinary People do Extraordinary Things," Jody Williams

- ◆ IQ (inquiry question about self): Has there been a time when you were called on to do something extraordinary? Or have you witnessed someone doing something extraordinary? What prompted you/them to do so? What was the result?
- ◆ CQ (critical question about text): According to Jody Williams, what prompts people to do extraordinary things?
- ◆ Activity: Write your own "This I Believe" essay about what you believe in.

Text: "Letter from a Birmingham City Jail," Martin Luther King Jr.

- ◆ CQ: What methods does Martin Luther King Jr. advocate for in his letter? Why? Evaluate their effectiveness.

Text: "Indifference," Elie Wiesel

- ◆ IQ: Has there been a time when you were indifferent and now wish you would have reacted differently? What was the result?
- ◆ CQ: According to Elie Wiesel, what are the causes and consequences of indifference?

Allegiance and Survival
Text: *Night*, Elie Wiesel

- ◆ CQ: What was the cost of allegiance during the Holocaust?
- ◆ CQ: How did the need to survive impact one's allegiance?
- ◆ CQ: Analyze the causes and consequences of genocide. Why do they recur through history and what do you propose can be done to stop them?

Allegiance and Duty (self, state)
Text: *Bhagavad Gita*

- ◆ IQ: To what/whom do you have a duty?
- ◆ CQ: What is Arjuna's conflict?
- ◆ CQ: How does Krishna help Arjuna reconcile his resistance to fight? What might this reflect about ancient Indian beliefs?
- ◆ Essay: When faced with the decision to go into battle, what should Arjuna do? Why?
- ◆ Activity: Mock Therapy Session between Arjuna and Krishna.

Allegiance and Duty (family, self, state)
Text: *Antigone*, Sophocles

- ◆ CQ: What factors influence Antigone's decision to bury her brother?
- ◆ CQ: What might the play reflect about Greek beliefs and society of the time?
- ◆ Activity: Storyboard the play with illustrations and key quotations.
- ◆ Essay: How does Antigone reconcile her conflicting allegiances? What does Antigone feel a duty to?
- ◆ Essay: Compare and contrast the beliefs of ancient Greece with those of ancient India, as reflected in *The Bhagavad Gita* and *Antigone*. What do you suspect was the motivation in encouraging such beliefs as they relate to society?

- ◆ Write a letter to Antigone from Krishna in *The Gita*, advising her of what to do based on his beliefs.
- ◆ Performance: *Antigone* Rock Musical. Recreate the play based on your storyboard interpretation. Choose music to accompany the scenes.
- ◆ AP Literature corresponding prompt: Many works of literature deal with political or social issues. Choose a novel or play that focuses on a political or social issue. Then write an essay in which you analyze how the author uses literary elements to explore this issue and explain how the issue contributes to the meaning of the work as a whole. Do not merely summarize the plot.

Redemption
Text: *The Kite Runner*, Khaled Hosseini

- ◆ IQ: What was the moment that made you into who you are today? Or, if you don't have a moment yet, what has made you into who you are today? To what extent do your race/culture/gender/sexuality identifications shape your worldview?
- ◆ CQ: Describe the narrator's relationship with either Hassan or his father.
- ◆ CQ: How might Amir's longing for his father's love impact his friendship with Hassan?
- ◆ CQ: How does Amir react during and after the incident? Why?
- ◆ CQ: How does Hassan choose to act towards Amir following the incident? Why?
- ◆ CQ: Is there a way to be good again for Amir? Is redemption possible? Does he want it? Is he willing to do what it takes to achieve it? Is he capable of it?
- ◆ CQ: What do the characters stand for (Amir, Hassan, Baba, Assef)?
- ◆ CQ: To what extent are Amir and Hassan foils of each other?
- ◆ CQ: How do Amir and Hassan's cultural identifications shape their worldviews?

- CQ: How does the literary technique of using flashbacks enhance the telling of the story?
- CQ: How does Amir's knowledge that Hassan is his half-brother influence his decisions?
- CQ: How is Amir's path to redemption connected to Baba's?
- CQ: Does Amir find redemption?

Essay Options

1. SAT corresponding prompt: We are often encouraged to top worrying about making mistakes and advised not to dwell on those we have already made. But without analyzing mistakes—decisions and actions that made a project fail, for instance—how can anyone be successful? Besides, there are some well-known mistakes others have made that seem worth studying carefully. Perhaps these mistakes could have been prevented if those responsible had been more concerned about making mistakes in the first place. Assignment: Do people have to pay attention to mistakes in order to make progress? Plan and write an essay in which you develop your point of view on this issue. Support your position with reasoning and examples taken from your reading, studies, experience, or observations.

2. AP Literature corresponding prompt: In a novel by William Styron, a father tells his son that life "is a search for justice." Choose a character from a novel or play who responds in some significant way to justice or injustice. Then write a well-developed essay in which you analyze the character's understanding of justice, the degree to which the character's search for justice is successful, and the significance of this search for the work as a whole.

Here I Stand Mental Health Research and Video Project

As the culminating project for our unit, choose an issue that needs attention and stand for it.

Part 1: Research to Develop a Solid Understanding of Your Issue

1. Choose an issue to stand for. Sample topics: bullying, mental health, education, immigration, poverty, domestic violence, gender rights, human trafficking, environment.
2. Develop a research question that does not have a clear answer and can be researched. *Include how the issue impacts mental health.* Sample question: What is the relationship between bullying and depression?
3. Research at least 3–5 different types of credible sources to find information about your topic. Examples of credible sources include: reputable magazine and newspaper articles, university research papers, books. List 2–3 pieces of evidence from each source and develop a works cited page using MLA Format.

Part II: 3–5-Page Research Paper Answering Your Question

1. Write a 3–5-page research paper answering your question.
2. Format: Double-spaced, Times New Roman, 12 point font, 1 inch margins.
3. Include the works cited page for your research sources.

Part III: Video

Create a 3-minute video that utilizes creative storytelling to teach others about your issue. The format is open to documentary, public service announcement (PSA), narrative, digital photo essay/photovoice or other innovative explorations that involve filmmaking components. Include:

1. What is the issue?
2. What is your call to action to improve the situation?

3. How is this work connected to the local community (neighborhood/school/family)?
4. What organizations are already working on this issue?

Part V: Here I Stand Film Festival and Soapbox Presentation

Present your video along with a 5–7-minute presentation of your issue.

1. Include issue, why it's important, question, research findings, and ways others can get involved.
2. Introduce your film and give a conclusion after the film.
3. Prepare for any questions that may be asked.

Extra Options
Option 1: Take Action: Service and Interview

1. Identify a local organization that works in support of your issue.
2. Service. Do 3–5 hours of volunteer service at the organization. Call or email them first. Sample call script: "Good afternoon. I'm a high school student and I'm working on a project about _____. I'm interested in what you do at (their organization). Would it be possible if I came to your organization and volunteered and/or talked to someone to learn more about _____?"
3. Interview. Interview someone at the organization. Develop 10 or more questions ahead of time. Sample questions may include: "How did you get involved in____? What are some of the biggest challenges your organization faces? How do you envision the future of _____?"
4. Submit a one-page write-up of your interview and a brief, signed letter stating your completion of service.

Option 2: Create a Proposal for a School or Community Organization that Addresses Your Issue

1. Choose a Name.
2. Write a Vision Statement (what you will accomplish) and Mission Statement (how you will accomplish it).
3. Develop 3–5 Core Values: What characteristics does your organization embody.
4. Create a one-page proposal on what your organization will achieve and how you will achieve it. Include steps 1–3 in your proposal.

Option 3: Apply to be Part of our School Mental Health Team

Application Components:

1. Develop a plan of action for your issue to be implemented at school. Include a strategic and marketing plan.
2. Identify which individuals and stakeholders should be part of the team.
3. Create an assessment plan for how you would measure success.

Option 4: Enter a Contest to Magnify Your Voice

1. Find a relevant student contest to enter.
2. Modify your submission to fit needed project criteria.
3. Print submission verification form.

Thematic Unit 2: Times of Transition (Grades 11–12)

Unit Summary

Students will explore how and why individuals in literature, history, and life experience transitions. They will examine their own life transitions, and complete a culminating project in which they create a Transition Roadmap where they will address the elements of a successful transition. Through the unit, students will build skills in reading, writing, speaking, and listening, in a critical thinking, solutions-based, global competence framework.

Common Core State Standards

1. CCSS.ELA-LITERACY.RI.11-12.1 Cite strong and thorough textual evidence to support analysis of what the text says explicitly as well as inferences drawn from the text, including determining where the text leaves matters uncertain.
2. CCSS.ELA-LITERACY.W.11-12.1 Write arguments to support claims in an analysis of substantive topics or texts, using valid reasoning and relevant and sufficient evidence.
3. CCSS.ELA-LITERACY.SL.11-12.1 Initiate and participate effectively in a range of collaborative discussions (one-on-one, in groups, and teacher-led) with diverse partners on grades 11–12 topics, texts, and issues, building on others' ideas and expressing their own clearly and persuasively.

Students will explore a variety of global articles, books, texts, and film excerpts to discern the elements of a successful quest, and how and why individuals seek fulfillment of their goals.

Possible Texts

- ◆ *Metamorphosis*, Franz Kafka
- ◆ *The Piano Lesson*, August Wilson
- ◆ *Hamlet*, William Shakespeare
- ◆ *A Place for Us*, Fatima Farheen Mirza
- ◆ *How to be an Antiracist*, Ibram X. Kendi

- *A Taste of Power*, Elaine Brown
- *The Sweetness of Water*, Nathan Harris
- *One Flew Over the Cuckoo's Nest*, Ken Kesey
- *Tipping Point*, Malcom Gladwell
- *Daring Greatly*, Brené Brown
- *Pygmalion*, George Bernard Shaw
- Poems: "The Love Song of J. Alfred Prufrock," T.S. Eliot; "Poem for a Half-White College Student," Amiri Baraka
- Song: "Lose Yourself," Eminem
- Art: Jackson Pollack, Andy Warhol, Banksy
- Film*: Antwone Fisher*
- Historical Connection: Transitions in cities and communities. Technology and Globalization

Sample Learning Questions and Activities on Select Texts

Metamorphosis

Text: *Metamorphosis*, Franz Kafka. Possible Companion Text: *Pygmalion*, George Bernard Shaw

- IQ (inquiry question about self): If you could wake up changed into anything, what would it be?
- CQ (critical question about text): Character description: How does Gregor initially react to his change?
- CQ How does Gregor's family react to his change? Why? How does this compare or contrast to his reaction?
- CQ DO/SAY/FEEL Chart. Map out what the characters do, say, and feel through the story. Note changes. What is the significance to the meaning of the work as a whole?
- Essay: How do Gregor and his family transform through his story? What message might this reflect about 20th-century Europe? Why?
- Project: Write your own short story or children's book starting with the line: "When _____woke up one morning from unsettling dreams, he/she/they found herself/himself/themselves changed in his/her/their bed into a _____.''

The Past, Present, and Future
Text: *The Piano Lesson*, August Wilson

- ◆ IQ: Do you live in the past, present, or future? Which would you like to live in? Do you have an object that represents your past that you would not want to part with?
- ◆ CQ: Character description: Describe why/how each character lives in the past, present, or future.
- ◆ CQ: What does the piano represent to the characters? Should they sell it or keep it? Why?
- ◆ Essay: How does the piano help the characters either stay connected to their roots or progress to their future? Discuss the symbolic nature of the piano and what themes it reflects for the characters.
- ◆ SAT Essay Prompt: Too often, people fail to solve problems because they focus only on the problems, thinking that if they study a problem, it will eventually suggest its own solution. Instead, they should remember their past successes and retrace their steps by analyzing what they did or did not do in similar situations in the past. It is often said that there is no formula for success, but if people would only focus on repeating the specific actions that worked for them before, they would surely succeed again. Assignment: Are people likely to succeed by repeating actions that worked for them in the past? Plan and write an essay in which you develop your point of view on this issue. Support your position with reasoning and examples taken from your reading, studies, experience, or observations.

Internal and External Struggles
Text: *Hamlet*, William Shakespeare

- ◆ IQ: What are ten things that drive you crazy?
- ◆ CQ: Character description of Hamlet.
- ◆ CQ: What is the role and function of the Ghost in the play?
- ◆ CQ: What are the factors that cause Hamlet to change?

- ◆ CQ: Why does the Ghost return in Scene 3, Act 4? What is its significance?
- ◆ CQ: What transitions occur in the play? How does Shakespeare construct the transitions?
- ◆ CQ: What impact does Hamlet's transformation have on Ophelia? What larger meaning of the work is reflected in her response?
- ◆ Essay: What factors contribute to Hamlet's transition in the play? To what extent does Hamlet have control over his transition and actions?

Approaches to Life
Texts: "Lose Yourself," Eminem; "The Love Song of J. Alfred Prufrock," T.S. Eliot.

- ◆ CQ: How does J. Alfred Prufrock view love and life?
- ◆ CQ: How does Eminem approach life through his song?
- ◆ CQ Essay: Contrast the views on life that Eminem and J. Alfred Prufrock have. Evaluate how/why each text reflects larger societal themes and whose method is most effective for portraying his view on society.

Facing the Past
Film: *Antwone Fisher*

- ◆ IQ: How do you deal with challenges in your life?
- ◆ IQ: Evaluate your strengths in the following five foundations of success: purpose, adaptability, endurance resilience, relationships, resourcefulness
- ◆ CQ: What challenges does Antwone initially face? How does he deal with them? How does this start to change through his life?
- ◆ Essay: How does Antwone's approach to life change through the film? Which of the five foundations of success enables him to change?
- ◆ AP Literature corresponding prompt: "You can leave home all you want, but home will never leave you." — Sonsyrea Tate. Sonsyrea Tate's statement suggests that

"home" may be conceived of as a dwelling, a place, or a state of mind. It may have positive or negative associations, but in either case, it may have a considerable influence on an individual. Choose a novel or play in which a central character leaves home yet finds that home remains significant. Write a well-developed essay in which you analyze the importance of "home" to this character and the reasons for its continuing influence. Explain how the character's idea of home illuminates the larger meaning of the work.

Personal Stories

◆ Activity: What is your life transformation story? What was a moment in your life where you experienced a change that impacted the course of your life or your beliefs? How did you react to it? How did it change you? What did you learn from it?

Assessments

1. Create a rubric to evaluate who among the individuals studied this unit experienced the most successful transition. Evaluate rubric criteria as it applies to each individual.
2. Culminating Essay: Choose three of individuals studied to determine who had the strongest transition. Include in your response the elements of a successful transition, the factors that made that individual more successful than the others in his/her transition, and the implications of his/her transition.
3. Potential Projects: Transitions Children's Book, Transition Survival Guide, Mapping Transitions: Individuals, Families, Communities.

Thematic Unit 3: The Quest for Treasure (Grades 9–10)

Unit Summary

This unit is designed to teach students goal setting through the lens of individuals and characters studied. Students will explore themes such as goal setting and fulfillment, decision-making, methods of goal achievement, overcoming obstacles and the cost–benefit of goals. They will correspondingly build skills in target areas of reading, writing, speaking and listening through a critical thinking, solutions-based lens.

Common Core State Standards

1. CCSS.ELA-LITERACY.RI.11-12.1 Cite strong and thorough textual evidence to support analysis of what the text says explicitly as well as inferences drawn from the text.
2. CCSS.ELA-LITERACY.W.11-12.1 Write arguments to support claims in an analysis of substantive topics or texts, using valid reasoning and relevant and sufficient evidence.
3. CCSS.ELA-LITERACY.SL.11-12.1 Initiate and participate effectively in a range of collaborative discussions (one-on-one, in groups, and teacher-led) with diverse partners on grades 9–10 topics, texts, and issues, building on others' ideas and expressing their own clearly and persuasively.

Essential Questions

1. What is the importance of "treasure"/goals in life?
2. What does it mean to be successful?
3. What are strategies for goal fulfillment?
4. What are strategies to overcome obstacles that may stand in the way of success?

Possible Texts

◆ Poem: "The Road Not Taken," Robert Frost
◆ Poem: "Shoulders," Naomi Nye

- Poem: "Uphill," Christina Rossetti
- Non-Fiction: *7 Habits of Highly Effective Teens*, Sean Covey
- Non-Fiction: *The Best Advice I Ever Got*, Katie Couric
- *The Alchemist*, Paulo Coelho (introduction or entirety)
- *The Stranger*, Albert Camus
- *The Odyssey*, Homer
- *Know My Name*, Chanel Miller
- *The Vanishing Half*, Brit Bennett
- *Educated*, Tara Westover
- *My Grandmother's Hands*, Resmaa Manakem
- *Into the Wild*, Jon Krakauer
- Film: *Slumdog Millionaire*
- Short Story: "A Sound of Thunder," Ray Bradbury
- Poem: "Hold Fast to Dreams," Langston Hughes
- Play: *A Raisin in the Sun*, Lorraine Hansberry
- Art: Treasure
- Historical Connection: Current events. News (such as CNN10), identifying goals and methods in the stories.

Thematic Vocabulary

quest, pursuit, cache, decisions, objective, priority, cost, output, sustain, environment

Sample Learning Questions

- What does treasure or success mean to you? How can and will you attain it? What are some obstacles that might be in your path? How can you overcome them?
- What quest guides the actions of the characters or individuals?
- What do the characters/individuals learn through their journeys?
- According to Paolo Coelho's *The Alchemist*, what is the importance of a Personal Legend? How can it be achieved?

◆ How does the environmental landscape influence the journey of the characters?

◆ What is treasure in the texts/film? To whom? How does it change through time? How does treasure motivate the characters to reach their goals?

◆ What methods do the characters/individuals use to reach their goal? Whose is most effective and why?

◆ What must the characters/individuals sacrifice in order to achieve their goal? Why must they give up these things?

◆ Compare/contrast the beliefs that guide the characters through their quests.

◆ How do the characters/individuals overcome obstacles to achieving their goals?

◆ What role does the relationships with others have in the fulfillment of goals?

Sample Learning Activities

1. Read Robert Frost's poem "The Road Not Taken" and analyze his message alongside the other road poems of "Shoulders" and "Uphill." Students write and present their own imitation road poems. Can be made into a collective class poem book.

2. Review selections of the novel as a group, developing skills in quote finding and analysis around what it means to be on a quest.

3. Discussions on critical questions. Practice developing and presenting supported ideas on what makes a quest successful or not.

4. Examine newspapers or media for examples of people who are on a quest and how they achieved it. Include athlete stories on determination in the face of obstacles.

5. Explore the history of the countries that the book/films relate to. Break students into groups to identify the important quests of that country and report back to the class.

6. Mock discussion or Socratic seminar taking on personas of characters across book and film to discuss their personal quests.
7. TED Talk or NPR StoryCorps interview of a character or individual in the unit, highlighting what it means for that person to be on their quest.
8. Students write their own Personal Legend after reading the introduction to Paulo Coelho's *The Alchemist*.

Summative Assessments

1. Essay: Compare the quest of Santiago in *The Alchemist* with that of Jamal in *Slumdog Millionaire*. What motivates the characters through the development of their quests? How are they influenced by both their physical environment and the other characters to alter their journey? How and why do the characters either realize or fall short of their goal?
2. Project: Create a quest board game using the principles of a quest studied in this unit.
3. Project: Photographing Success. Photography project and presentation on what it means to be successful in a quest. Gallery walk display of student work in or outside of the classroom or school.

StoryCorps Interview Project

Interview someone to learn about their quest in life. Content and questions from website: http://storycorps.org

A StoryCorps interview is 40 minutes of uninterrupted time for meaningful conversation with a friend or loved one. What are the questions you want to ask and the memories you want to preserve? No matter how well you know your storyteller, a little preparation will improve the quality of your interview enormously. There are four basic steps:

1. *Welcome* (5 minutes): Provide some background information about the interview and project, explain what will happen during it and answer any questions.

2. *Interview* (40 minutes): Use your prepared question list (choose from the questions below or create your own), but remember they are just suggestions to get you started. Trust your instincts. When you hear something that moves you, ask more questions. Sometimes your storyteller will need "permission" to explore a certain topic; you can simply say "Tell me more." Feel free to ask questions in whatever order feels right, and don't let them constrain the conversation. Real moments are the best moments. Some tips for helping the conversation flow:
    *   Look at your storyteller's eyes. Stay interested and engaged
    *   Be yourself; you can laugh or even cry with your storyteller.
    *   Emotional questions like "how does this make you feel?" often elicit thoughtful responses. Don't be afraid to ask.
    *   Be curious and honest and keep an open heart.
    *   While you and your partner are talking, take notes, keep time, and monitor audio (if available).

3. *Photos* (5 minutes): Finally, take a photo of you and your interview partner, both together and separately.

4. *After the interview:* Summarize interview into a one-page overview of the main ideas discussed. Include the photo if possible.

Great Questions for Anyone

1. Who has been the most important person in your life? Can you tell me about him or her?
2. What was the happiest moment of your life? The saddest?
3. Who has been the biggest influence on your life? What lessons did that person teach you?
4. Who has been the kindest to you in your life?
5. What are the most important lessons you've learned in life?
6. What is your earliest memory?
7. What is your favorite memory of me?
8. Are there any funny stories your family tells about you that come to mind?
9. Are there any funny stories or memories or characters from your life that you want to tell me about?
10. What are you proudest of?
11. When in life have you felt most alone?
12. If you could hold on to one memory from your life forever, what would that be?
13. How has your life been different than what you'd imagined?
14. How would you like to be remembered?
15. Do you have any regrets?
16. What does your future hold?
17. What are your hopes for what the future holds for me? For my children?
18. If this was to be our very last conversation, is there anything you'd want to say to me?
19. For your great great grandchildren listening to this years from now: is there any wisdom you'd want to pass on to them? What would you want them to know?
20. Is there anything that you've never told me but want to tell me now?
21. Is there something about me that you've always wanted to know but have never asked?

Grandparents

1. Where did you grow up?
2. What was your childhood like?
3. Who were your favorite relatives?
4. Do you remember any of the stories they used to tell you?
5. How did you and grandma/grandpa meet?
6. What was my mom/dad like growing up?
7. Do you remember any songs that you used to sing to her/him? Can you sing them now?
8. Was she/he well-behaved?
9. What is the worst thing she/he ever did?
10. What were your parents like?
11. What were your grandparents like?
12. How would you like to be remembered?
13. Are you proud of me?

Parents

1. Do you remember what was going through your head when you first saw me?
2. How did you choose my name?
3. What was I like as a baby? As a young child?
4. Do you remember any of the songs you used to sing to me? Can you sing them now?
5. What were my siblings like?
6. What were the hardest moments you had when I was growing up?
7. If you could do everything again, would you raise me differently?
8. What advice would you give me about raising my own kids?
9. What are your dreams for me?
10. How did you meet mom/dad?
11. Are you proud of me?

Growing Up

1. When and where were you born?
2. Where did you grow up?
3. What was it like?
4. Who were your parents?
5. What were your parents like?
6. How was your relationship with your parents?
7. Did you get into trouble? What was the worst thing you did?
8. Do you have any siblings? What were they like growing up?
9. What did you look like?
10. How would you describe yourself as a child? Were you happy?
11. What is your best memory of childhood? Worst?
12. Did you have a nickname? How'd you get it?
13. Who were your best friends? What were they like?
14. How would you describe a perfect day when you were young?
15. What did you think your life would be like when you were older?
16. Do you have any favorite stories from your childhood?

School

1. Did you enjoy school?
2. What kind of student were you?
3. What would you do for fun?
4. How would your classmates remember you?
5. Are you still friends with anyone from that time in your life?
6. What are your best memories of grade school/high school/college/graduate school? Worst memories?
7. Was there a teacher or teachers who had a particularly strong influence on your life? Tell me about them.
8. Do you have any favorite stories from school?

Love and Relationships

1. Do you have a love of your life?
2. When did you first fall in love?
3. Can you tell me about your first kiss?
4. What was your first serious relationship?
5. Do you believe in love at first sight?
6. What lessons have you learned from your relationships?

Working

1. What do you do for a living?
2. Tell me about how you got into your line of work.
3. Do you like your job?
4. What did you think you were going to be when you grew up?
5. What did you want to be when you grew up?
6. What lessons has your work life taught you?
7. If you could do anything now, what would you do? Why?
8. Do you plan on retiring? If so, when? How do you feel about it?
9. Do you have any favorite stories from your work life?

Family Heritage

1. What is your ethnic background?
2. Where is your mom's family from? Where is your dad's family from?
3. Have you ever been there? What was that experience like?
4. What traditions have been passed down in your family?
5. Who were your favorite relatives?
6. Do you remember any of the stories they used to tell you?
7. What are the classic family stories? Jokes? Songs?

Remembering A Loved One

1. What was your relationship to _____?
2. Tell me about _____.
3. What is your first memory of _____?
4. What is your best memory of _____?
5. What is your most vivid memory of _____?
6. What did _____ mean to you?
7. Are you comfortable/can you talk about _____'s death? How did _____ die?
8. What has been the hardest thing about losing _____?
9. What would you ask _____ if _____ were here today?
10. What do you miss most about _____?
11. How do you think _____ would want to be remembered?
12. Can you talk about the biggest obstacles _____ overcame in life?
13. Was there anything you and _____ disagreed about, fought over, or experienced some conflict around?
14. What about _____ makes you smile?
15. What was your relationship like?
16. What did _____ look like?
17. Did you have any favorite jokes _____ used to tell?
18. Do you have any stories you want to share about _____?
19. What were _____'s hopes and dreams for the future?
20. Is there something about _____ that you think no one else knows?
21. How are you different now than you were before you lost _____?
22. What is the image of _____ that persists?
23. Do you have any traditions to honor _____?
24. What has helped you the most in your grief?
25. What are the hardest times?

University Mindfulness Course Syllabus

Introduction to Mindfulness
Units: 2.0

Course Description
This experiential course is an introduction to mindfulness. Through it, students will learn the principles of practice, develop their own meditation practice, and apply principles to daily life. They will learn strategies to skillfully work with thoughts, emotions, and sensations, while developing their capacity to enhance mind–body awareness of present-moment experience. They will study theory and research in the field of mindfulness and the emerging science that shows promising, beneficial effects for physical and mental health and well-being. This course is designed for beginners and is also suitable for those with experience who want to refine their practice. Classes consist of a combination of lecture, practice, and discussion.

Learning Outcomes

1. Synthesize theory, practice, and research in mindfulness and apply understanding to individual practice.
2. Develop and sustain personal meditation practice.
3. Investigate mind–body awareness and connection and apply principles to enhance capacity for presence, connection, openness, and curiosity in experiences.
4. Describe and apply mindfulness principles to skillfully cultivate focus and concentration, including as they relate to working with emotions, thoughts, and sensations.
5. Describe and apply mindfulness principles as they relate to self-regulation in navigating difficult emotions and thoughts, including stress and anxiety.
6. Identify and apply techniques to skillfully cultivate emotions of well-being, such as kindness, compassion, joy, and equanimity.

7. Apply mindful awareness in daily life, including as it relates to:
   a. clarity in decision-making and problem solving to skillfully respond, rather than react, to complex situations.
   b. interpersonal relationships and relational mindfulness practices of active listening and mindful communication.
   c. navigating change, time management, and exploring what it means to have a conscious and purposeful relationship with technology.

Acknowledgement

Though our program here is secular, it is with an acknowledgement for the roots mindfulness has in Buddhist philosophy, which emerged in the context of an ancient India where Hinduism, Jainism, yoga, asceticism, and other traditions were practiced. Certain practices and ideas have evolved and been carried across time and geography and have been adapted here for a foundational, interdisciplinary study. We would also like to acknowledge and honor the ancestral and unceded land of the Tongva people that our university sits on. For at least 9,000 years, they stewarded the land we call Southern California along with their neighbors, the Chumash, Tataviam, Kitanemuk, Serrano, Cahuilla, Payomkawichum, Acjachemen, Ipai-Tipai, Kumeyaay, and Quechan peoples. To learn more about the history of these indigenous lands: https://dornsife.usc.edu/hist/land-acknowledgement/

Required Course Book

Mindfulness for Young Adults: Tools to Thrive in School and Life, by Linda Yaron Weston

Available in print and e-book
20% off if purchased through Routledge using code FLR40.
On reserve with USC Library
Also available at USC Bookstore and on Amazon.

Communication

I encourage students to reach out by email and will try to respond as soon as possible, and within 48 hours.

Reflection and Evaluation

Reflection is an integral part of the learning and teaching process. As such, you will complete a series of reflections on your practice through the course. We will also complete mid- and end-of-course evaluations for the course so that it can best serve the needs of students. Please feel free to also communicate feedback to me through the semester in person or by email.

Online Etiquette (if online)

Your presence and engagement are as important online as in a physical classroom. Please plan to have screens on when possible and be on time to class. Once class has begun, it may take time to be admitted if meditation is in progress. Mute when not speaking to minimize background noise.

Grades

The impact of your practice will be felt in how much effort, time, and awareness you choose to invest in it. Grades are based on your willingness to show up for your personal and class practice and are based on your approach to the following criteria:

1. Presence: time and awareness to show up for your practice
2. Effort: diligence and precision with which you practice
3. Curiosity: growth through a nonjudgmental approach
4. Kindness: choosing gentleness and patience over harshness towards body, mind, and practice

All work is due on the assigned date and is to be typed and submitted to Blackboard. Format: submit as a Word or PDF document, double-spaced, Times New Roman, 12-point font, 1" margins,

MLA format. Due dates under course outline. Assignments included in course book *Mindfulness for Young Adults: Tools to Thrive in School and Life.*

♦ **60 Points**: Attend class and participate in sessions. 4 points for each week. It is the responsibility of each student to accurately sign in. Participation is an essential component of this course and serves to deepen student inquiry and reflection of the course material. Students need to be present in class to earn participation points. There will be an absence make-up opportunity in Module 5.

♦ **20 Points Each (100 points total): 5 Module Reflection Forms (for each of the 5 Modules).** They include:

• <u>Daily personal meditation practice log</u>. 5–10 minutes per day recommended time Modules 1, 2 (weeks 1–4); 10–15 minutes per day Modules 3, 4 (weeks 5–8); 15-20+ minutes/day Module 5 (weeks 9–15). Or, you may increase depth by a self-chosen amount of minutes each week. You are welcome to use an app, guided meditations, or break up the time through the day.

• <u>Rubric criteria</u>: 8–10 points for meditation practice (presence, effort); 2–2.5 points for each of the written responses (thorough, reflective).

• <u>Workbook prompts</u>. Choose 2 questions from the module to answer.

• <u>Class reflection prompts</u>. Submit a reflection from class each module. Can be typed or submitted as a picture included in your document.

• <u>Outside meditation class</u>. Attend a meditation class outside ours. Include reflection in Module 4 (week 8) form.

♦ **40 Points. Mindfulness in Daily Life Group Strategy and Presentation.**

1. <u>Choose an area/topic</u> in mindfulness you're interested in exploring with a group in Week 4. Areas of daily life can include relationships and

communication, mindful eating, self-care and self-compassion, mindful technology use, mindful learning, mindful decision-making, mindful movement, or social justice.

2. <u>Choose a mindfulness strategy to apply to an area of daily life</u> you'd like to try out <u>regularly for 5 weeks</u> (daily or minimum 3 times per week). While groups will choose a shared topic to explore as a community, they may all employ different strategies within it. You are welcome to explore apps that track progress or enhance your experience.

3. Organize a group in-class 15-minute per group <u>presentation</u> on your mindfulness topic and strategy. Include relevant research behind it (from credible, evidence-based sources; MLA format), reflections on how your strategy went, recommendations, or next steps. Presentations should be cooperative with each group member speaking, and interactive in nature (the class participates in the particular technique), and be visually displayed (ie. PowerPoint, Prezy, etc.).

   - <u>Rubric criteria</u>: 8 points for each of the following:
   - Content: clearly and concisely convey thoughtful ideas and examples
   - Application: Understanding and application of mindfulness principles
   - Voice: volume, clarity, emotion
   - Stance: body language, eye contact, presence
   - Style: effort, creativity, organization, applicability, interactivity, collaboration

◆ **75 Points. Online Exam**. Based on content from reading, class content, and discussions. Be sure to stay current on course reading and material, as not all content on exam will be discussed in class.

◆ **25 Points. Meditation Final Reflection**. Rubric Criteria: 5 points for each: Thorough, reflective, creative, understands and applies principles of practice.

Grading Scale

There are 300 total points possible. The overall grading scale is as follows

A 282 / A– 270 / B+ 265 / B 260 / B– 255 / C+ 250 / C 245 / C– 240 / D 235

Course Outline

Date	Topic
Week 1 Module 1: Principles	What is mindfulness?; principles of practice Mindfulness and identity **Begin daily meditation practice (5–10 minutes/day)** Workbook: Module 1: 1.0, 1.1
Week 2	Effort and concentration; anchor Emerging science of mindfulness Technique: STOP: Stop, Take a breath, Observe, Proceed* **Due Sunday: Module 1 Reflection Form** (includes mindfulness article) Workbook: Module 1: 1.2, 1.3, 1.4
Week 3 Module 2: Body	Mind–body awareness and connection Conscious breathing Technique: Body scan **Share an article about mindfulness or meditation** Workbook: Module 2: 2.0, 2.1
Week 4	Standing meditation, walking, and mindful movement* Mindful eating Choose mindfulness in daily life groups **Due Sunday: Module 2 Reflection Form** (includes daily life area selection) Workbook: Module 2: 2.2, 2.3, 2.4
Week 5 Module 3: Heart	Working with emotions: noticing and processing Compassion, kindness Technique: RAIN: Recognize, Allow, Investigate, Nonidentify, Nurture **Deepen daily meditation practice (10–15 minutes/day)** Workbook: Module 3: 3.0, 3.1
Week 6	Working with difficult emotions; mindfulness and mental health Forgiveness, equanimity; Joy, gratitude* **Due Sunday: Module 3 Reflection Form** (includes midsemester evaluation) Workbook: Module 3: 3.2, 3.3

Week 7 Module 4: Mind	Working with thoughts: observation and visualization techniques Uncertainty and anxiety Workbook: Module 4: 4.0, 4.1
Week 8	Resilience and post-traumatic growth Identity and social consciousness* **Due Sunday: Module 4 Reflection Form** (includes outside meditation class) Workbook: Module 4: 4.2, 4.3
Week 9 Module 5: Daily Life	Mindful communication Relational mindfulness; active listening and speaking **Deepen daily meditation practice 15–20+ minutes/day** Workbook: Module 5: 5.0, 5.1
Week 10	Mindfulness in decision-making*; consent Balancing time and priorities; technology Workbook: Module 5: 5.2
Week 11	Coping with change, loss, and impermanence Mindfulness and success **Due Sunday: Module 5 Reflection Form** (includes book reflection and make-up) Workbook: Module: 5: 5.3, 5.4
Week 12	**Due: Presentations (in class)**
Week 13	Debrief presentations and review modules Practice: open awareness* **Due Sunday: Online Exam** (Window Friday noon–Sunday midnight)
Week 14	Practice: open awareness*
Week 15	Closing and next steps End-of-Semester Evaluation **Due last day of class midnight: Final Reflection**

* indicates immersive meditation practice

Appendix B

Learner Statements

Situating themselves at the center of their education, high school seniors explored the essential question "What does it mean for you to be a learner?" They wrote learner statements which were then included in a class blog and book. Artwork and statements were showcased in an exhibition at the U.S. Department of Education in Washington, D.C. Included here is a selection of their voices and art. Real names are included on student artwork.

Growth Mindset

"A learner is someone who makes mistakes, learns from those mistakes, and progresses from them. A learner gains knowledge and understands. A learner excels and prevails to be the best that they can be in life. Learners break down information and analyze words of what they are trying to learn. They make questions and they make answers. Most of all, they question everything until they gain the truth. They reason with knowledge and apply all of what they know into skills. What makes us all learners is that we are all students of life."

—Sam

"To be a learner is to be able to accept failures and work hard to try again. I believe that failing is another chance to do something right. Accepting failure is always a hard thing to swallow, but if failure is taken as a motivation to be successful then failure can lead to success. Learning is a chance to acquire new knowledge and perception. I believe that everyone is a lifelong learner because there is no limitation on knowledge, and it is never too soon or too late to learn something."

—Danny

FIGURE B.1 *Super Scholars*, Iris Hernandez

Resilience

"To be a learner means to be a survivor. I strongly believe that as human beings, we cannot progress in life without an education. … To be a learner is to look at life and the world through a more scholarly lens. I am capable of understanding things in depth and to fully appreciate the values they bring. I know for a fact that my character is sustained by knowledge. With the tools I've learned from school, I am able live through any circumstance. Anyone can survive day by day starved without some form of intelligence. However, when we feed on knowledge, we're growing our strength to roam freely around the world."

—**Manuel**

"There have been many events in my life that have made me want to quit trying to achieve a successful life because it was the easier way out, but I realize that learning happens whether you think it's a choice or not. ... It's up to me to choose what path I want to take and how far I want to expand my learning experiences. In order for me to understand the abilities that come with being a learner, I must have discipline to realize what the truth is that I am facing at the moment and what my choices are, in order to make the choice that will help me grow as an individual."

—Flor

Power and Freedom

"Being a learner to me means having power. Having power in this country means having knowledge. Gaining knowledge means going to college and getting a degree. As a person you are not able to gain knowledge if you do not push yourself to succeed. You are able to use your knowledge in the streets and use it for your protection."

—Benito

"As a learner, I have taken every opportunity to grow and learn about my community. I search for ways to expand my knowledge beyond classroom lessons. Knowledge is the key to my success, and without it, I am nothing. To be a learner means to be free. There are children in the world who grow to be ignorant, keeping them from the truth. To be a learner is to seek out the truth in life and explore the infinite possibilities of who I can be. To be a learner is to be me. Knowledge is given to us because we are the future."

—Alba

FIGURE B.2 *Restricted Growth,* Rubi Torres

Community Responsibility

"As a learner I feel the responsibility to share my knowledge with my peers and anyone willing to learn more. I have a commitment to help my brothers and even my older sister if I know something that she may not, because we are all learners and each learner may know a certain subject more than others. My responsibility to my siblings is what drives me to learn more so that I'll be able to better help them with their education. Learners have a sense of always wanting to strive for more and help others feel educated. We are all learners and we all help each other benefit from one another."

—**Maria**

"I study so I can gain the knowledge to find solutions to reform the issues of my community … To be a learner, it requires hardships, hard work, and self-confidence. Without these three components, being a learner loses its purpose, and the goals and dreams will be merely just unreachable thoughts. It is my duty as a learner to have the responsibility for my own education and to put all my efforts in achieving the greatest. As a learner, I endeavor to gain new knowledge as well as teach others the wisdom I have, so someday every individual can be educated."

—**Francisco**

Quest for Knowledge

"My main mission in life is to gain as much knowledge as possible. To me, knowledge is the best power one can have to bring about any real transformations in the world. As an avid learner, my true purpose of education lies in the journey of learning, not the final graduation. My final certificate of the academic success lies not in a piece of paper, but in the self-satisfaction that I have utilized the available resources to gain as much knowledge as I possibly can, because that will give me the optimum possibility to cause any change of significant impact while contributing to the legacy of knowledge I have always coveted."

—**Benjamin**

"To be a learner means to have a hunger for knowledge. The easiest way to get a first bite is through education. Schools feed our students intelligence, whether the children are aware of it or not. It has been in my experience that the best way one can ever attain wisdom, is by feeding on every bite of knowledge he or she can. At an early age, I became exposed to visual arts, which brought me a key to unlock the door that led me to a beautiful world I soon longed to be a part of. My earliest memory of art was in elementary school. 'Take out your pencils and draw anything.' I looked around and saw everyone drawing. In that moment I felt overwhelmed because in front of me stood a white sheet of paper and a pencil. The possibilities were endless. I fell in love with art that day. ... I soaked it all in."

—Diego

Curiosity and Openness

"To be a learner, one has to be willing to be open to new ideas and a way of thinking. Be willing to attain new experiences. As a learner I have learned that you have to work with knowledge to be to use it for yourself because when you fight against it, it can fight against you too."

—Carmen

"A learner is a person who is driven to find things out and ask questions to seek answers. He or she observes, interprets, and analyzes his or her environment in order to comprehend the situation. When the learner finds the answer to questions, they extend the idea on how it is important to the real world and/or why it is important. Every individual is a learner from birth until the end of a lifespan. Growing up as a toddler, we learn from curiosity. As we see our mother put a hot bowl of soup on the table, we approach it and use one of our five unique senses. We touch the bowl only to realize it is hot and never do it again. As a learner, we take risks to try out new things and persist through the situation."

—Marco

Appendix C

Recommended Books for Further Study

Resilience, Courage, and Compassion

1. *Between the World and Me*, Ta-Nehisi Coates
2. Daring *Greatly: How the Courage to Be Vulnerable Transforms the Way We Live, Love, Parent, and Lead*, Brené Brown
3. *Educated*, Tara Westover
4. *Grit: The Power of Passion and Perseverance*, Angela Duckworth
5. *Know My Name: A Memoir*, Chanel Miller
6. *The Mindful Path to Self-Compassion: Freeing Yourself from Destructive Thoughts and Emotions*, Christopher Germer
7. *Presence: Bringing Your Boldest Self to Your Biggest Challenges*, Amy Cuddy
8. *Quiet: The Power of Introverts in a World That Can't Stop Talking*, Susan Cain
9. *Radical Candor: Be a Kick-Ass Boss Without Losing Your Humanity*, Kim Scott

Habits, Motivation, and Willpower

10. *Drive: The Surprising Truth About What Motivates Us*, Daniel Pink
11. *Flow: The Psychology of Optimal Experience*, Mihály Csíkszentmihályi
12. *How to be an Antiracist*, Ibram X. Kendi
13. *The Power of Habit: Why We Do What We Do in Life and Business*, Charles Duhigg
14. *The Seven Habits of Highly Effective People*, Stephen Covey
15. *Thinking, Fast and Slow*, Daniel Kahneman
16. *The Willpower Instinct: How Self-Control Works, Why It Matters, and What You Can Do to Get More of It*, Kelly McGonigal
17. *Willpower: Rediscovering the Greatest Human Strength*, Roy Baumeister and John Tierney

Happiness and Well-Being

18. *Happier: Learn the Secrets to Daily Joy and Lasting Fulfillment*, Tal Ben-Sharer
19. *The Happiness Advantage: The Seven Principles of Positive Psychology that Fuel Success and Performance at Work*, Shawn Anchor
20. *The How of Happiness: A New Approach to Getting the Life You Want*, Sonja Lyubomirsky
21. *How to Have a Good Day: Harness the Power of Behavioral Science to Transform Your Working Life*, Caroline Webb
22. *The Happiness Hypothesis: Finding Modern Truth in Ancient Wisdom*, Jonathan Haidt
23. *Flourish: A Visionary New Understanding of Happiness and Well-being*, Martin Seligman

Mental Health, Emotions, and Stress

24. *The Body Keeps Score: Body, Mind, and Brain in the Healing of Trauma*, Bessel van der Kolk
25. *How Emotions are Made*, Lisa Feldman Barrett
26. *My Grandmother's Hands: Racialized Trauma and the Pathway to Mending Our Hearts and Bodies*, Resmaa Menakem
27. *Set Boundaries, Find Peace: A Guide to Reclaiming Yourself*, Nedra Glover Tawwab
28. *The Telomere Effect: A Revolutionary Approach to Living Younger, Healthier, Longer*, Elissa Epel and Elizabeth Blackburn
29. *The Upside of Stress: Why Stress Is Good for You, and How to Get Good at It*, Kelly McGonigal
30. *The Upward Spiral: Using Neuroscience to Reverse the Course of Depression, One Small Change at a Time*, Alex Korb

Mindfulness

31. *The Inner Work of Racial Justice*, Rhonda Magee
32. *Insight Meditation*, Joseph Goldstein
33. *Mindfulness for Young Adults: Tools to Thrive in School and Life*, Linda Yaron Weston
34. *Mindfulness in Plain English*, Bhante Gunaratana

35. *Mindful of Race: Transforming Racism from the Inside Out*, Ruth King
36. *A Path with Heart*, Jack Kornfield
37. *Peace is Every Step*, Thich Nhat Hanh
38. *Teaching Mindfulness to Empower Adolescents*, Matthew Brensilver, JoAnna Hardy, Oren Jay Sofer
39. *True Refuge* by Tara Brach

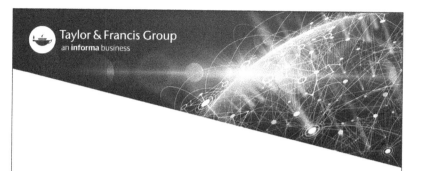